MARRIAGE
FOR
BETTER
OR FOR
WORSE

Diana R. & David E. Garland

BROADMAN PRESS
Nashville, Tennessee

4254-39
ISBN: 0-8054-5439-X

Dewey Decimal Classification: 306.8
Subject Heading: MARRIAGE

Library of Congress Catalog Card Number: 88-24207
Printed in the United States of America

Library of Congress Cataloging-in-Publication Data

Garland, Diana S. Richmond, 1950-
 Marriage: for better or for worse?

 (The Bible and personal crisis)
 1. Marriage—Religious aspects—Christianity.
I. Garland, David E. II. Title. III. Series.
BV835.G375 1989   248.4   88-24207
ISBN 0-8054-5439-X

Acknowledgments

We would like to express our appreciation to the Faculty Scholarship Development Program of The Southern Baptist Theological Seminary, which has been funded by the Lilly Endowment, Incorporated. They provided resources for Diana to be relieved of teaching responsibilities for a month in order to begin this manuscript. We are also grateful to Dr. Edward Thornton, who has been most helpful and encouraging in editing our work.

Contents

1

What's Happening to Marriages?

Americans have one of the highest marriage rates in the world; we believe in marriage. Although people nowadays wait until they are somewhat older to marry than they did twenty years ago (Melville, 1980), about 96 percent of Americans do marry at some point in their lives (Saxton, 1980). If you ask the average American to list the ingredients of a good life, most would place being happily married near the top. Even 80 percent of those who divorce marry again (Visher & Visher, 1979). This indicates that they still believe in marriage. Marriage can work, they think, if it is with the right partner. The trouble is that hopes about marriage can set us up for trouble.

Things That Can Trouble Marriages

We Expect Too Much of Marriage

What is it that Americans expect in marriage that makes it so important to them? Americans look for marriage to do something for them that no other relationship can do. The average American believes that when they tie the knot with someone they love, this person will always accept them for who they are, will always love them and listen to them, and will stand by them for the rest of their lives. They will never be lonely and will always be secure.

7

Most people want to put their faith in something permanent and beautiful, something to which they can give their lives. In the United States, for many persons that something is a marriage to the right partner (Elkind, 1981). A good marriage, they hope, will give meaning and purpose to their lives. I may be mistreated by the world; but if I have the right partner, I can face anything. A good marriage supposedly offers a secure harbor where we will find perpetual love and joy.

Our culture has almost made an idol out of marriage. We worry as a nation over rising divorce rates, because we have placed our faith and hope for the future not in God but in the American family. We believe that the most important relationship in life is with the marital partner. Some seem to believe that if they can find the right person as a partner, everything else in their lives will fall in place. The problem is that no marriage can live up to these hopes. But because this is what many expect from their marriage, they feel restless and unhappy when it fails to deliver. Marriage may become a hurricane on the open seas rather than a safe harbor. At times, marriage may make us feel more lonely than if we were alone, when the one to whom we are supposed to be so close does not seem to understand our feelings or even care about them. When these things happen, people often assume that they married the wrong person, that they were not meant for one another after all. They do not stop to think that what they expected of marriage was unrealistic.

We Expect Marriage to Help Us Reach
Our Greatest Potential as Persons

American marriage is not only supposed to keep us from being lonely; it is also supposed to help us become all that we can be. We want to be "self-actualized." To be self-actualized means you have fulfilled all of your potential. The model of self-actualization shows up in favorite television characters and articles in popular magazines that tell us how to improve ourselves. Self-actualized persons stay physically fit, arising before dawn to jog three miles or do aerobic workouts in front of a videocassette tape of a movie star. They then dress in clothes carefully chosen to fit their coloring type and eat a high-fiber breakfast designed to lower cholesterol and fat. They spend the day at a job that is challenging and serves humanity in some important way. Evenings are spent in satisfying activities with spouse and children. Self-actualized persons have creative hobbies, some of which they share with close friends, and others with marital partners. Sex is a time of intimate sharing which meets the needs of both and becomes more creative and meaningful as the relationship matures.

If we put this description in a series of pictures and asked people to circle what is wrong, they might have difficulty finding anything to mark. We would all like to have this kind of life. If we were to ask them to point out how this differs from their own life, however, the pencils would be more active. This is our point. Even a good marriage cannot ensure that partners will live according to the ideal that many Americans have. Yes, marriage may encourage us to grow as individuals. But marriage may also block the path to individual achievement.

The focus of marriage in the Bible is not on self-actualization but on the sacrifice required of marriage partners. When we marry, we commit ourselves to live loyally and lovingly for the rest of our lives in a future we cannot yet see. The families we grew up in are no longer the center of our lives. From the beginning, marriage has been the reason for leaving father and mother (Gen. 2:24). Yet we do not leave to go our individual way but to go with this new partner. The choices we make together in life will be different from those we would make if we had only ourselves to think about. Every aspect of our life bears the mark of our commitment to one another.

Let us return to our example of the ideal "self-actualized" life and picture how it might work out in the marriages of many people today. Husband prepares to go for an early morning jog only to learn that Wife has to go to work early this morning, and someone has to stay with the children to get them ready for school. He skips the jogging and slaps together peanut butter and jelly sandwiches for the lunch boxes. Then, he scurries off to work. Although his job is interesting, Husband would like very much to accept the promotion he has been offered. To take the new job, though, would mean a move to a distant city with much longer hours and more travel away from home. Wife does not want to leave her own work, and neither would be happy with the large amount of time away from home. This would put the responsibility for the children almost entirely on Wife. After work, Wife and Husband take the children to a fast-food restaurant for hamburgers before the Little League game. Their dinner talk focuses on what to do about the washing machine that is on the fritz: should we pay to have it repaired or simply buy a new one? By the time both drop in bed exhausted at the end of the day, one or both have little energy for lovemaking. If they decide to make love, it is often a tender but brief time in which they share closeness in much the same pattern as they have all the years of their married life.

This picture differs from the first one. It is not a troubled picture; but when placed alongside the "ideal," it might seem a little less than perfect. The lives of Husband and Wife are probably much different from what they would choose if they had only themselves and their own growth as individuals to think about. But they have gladly chosen to make sacrifices for the sake of their marriage covenant.

It may be the case that marriage will help one to reach full potential and use of one's talents. With the encouragement and support of our life partner, we can risk to do things we would not have had the courage or security to try on our own. On the other hand, marriage also requires that we sacrifice some of our individual dreams because of our commitment to one another. Paul recognized this; marriage, he said, brings with it "worldly troubles" (1 Cor. 7:28). Partners are not free to face life with a private purpose, even if that purpose is serving the Lord. Instead, they must be concerned about one another's needs. The husband is anxious to please his wife, and the wife is anxious to please her husband. Their interests are divided and sacrifices must be made (vv. 32-35).

Marriages Have Fewer Forces to Hold Them Intact

Americans expect so much of marriage; but when it fails to measure up to expectations, there is little nowadays to hold a marriage together. This contrasts sharply with the past. It has only been in this century that personal fulfillment and happiness have become the keys for gauging the success of a marriage. For our great-great-grandparents, divorce would have been almost unthinkable, unless one of the partners had been openly unfaithful. Even then, most marriages endured, especially if the husband was the guilty partner. It is not that marriages were happier or more fulfilling in the past when divorce was so rare; other forces came into play that kept a husband and wife together.

First, marriage partners were frequently business partners. They needed one another to survive. Both farms and businesses were usually run by the family. Work and homelife were not separate. Husbands and wives therefore depended on one another for more than just emotional support; they needed one another to survive economically. For example, in colonial and frontier America, the wife spun the thread, wove the cloth, and made clothes; she churned butter and preserved all the family's food; she butchered livestock and cared for the dairy cattle and chickens; she made candles and soap; and she made medicinal potions and cared for the sick. When she was needed in the family business or in the fields during harvesting or planting, she worked beside her husband. We can see this same pattern of economic cooperation between husband and wife in the Bible. The model wife, according to Proverbs, contributes to the economic well-being of the family. She buys a field, plants a vineyard, and sells what she makes for a profit (Prov. 31:10-31; see also Jer. 31:22).

Second, because women were not considered equal under the law, they faced real physical hardship if they were divorced. Men, on the other hand, faced social disgrace for abandoning their family. In addition to this, the law of the land and church doctrine made it difficult to divorce. Before "no-fault" divorce laws, most couples had to prove infidelity or specific cruelty in order to obtain a divorce. Although different churches have varying views today, it has only been recently that churches have begun to recognize the legitimacy of divorce for grounds other than unfaithfulness.

Finally, the family was the major protection people had against whatever crises the world threw at them; and marriage was the heart of the family. Life insurance, health insurance plans, hospitals, nursing homes, Social Security, and retirement funds were nonexistent. In sickness, in financial need, or in old age, people had to rely on their families. Divorce tore holes in the web of family ties that provided this support. Therefore, the demands of family and society forced people to stay married.

Most of these outside forces that kept couples together in the past are gone today. Work is no longer family based; most have individual careers. If both spouses work, they pool their incomes, but they usually do not have to have one another as business partners in order to do their work. Although working women, on the average, earn far less money than men, they can survive alone. Couples today can also divorce about as easily as they can marry. Laws now accept irreconcilable differences as grounds for divorce. Although most churches still frown on divorce, few actually withdraw fellowship from those who divorce. They might empty out fast if they did! Finally, people feel more protected as individuals buy life insurance, health insurance, professional medical care, and retirement plans and retirement facilities. We no longer need to be married, or even be a part of a family, to survive in our society.

We can demonstrate how marriage today differs from the past by imagining it as a box. The love and commitment of the spouses to one another and their happiness and fulfillment as persons are the glue that holds the box together. In the past, the box was also wrapped tightly with reinforced packing tape—the tape of needing one another to survive economically, the tape of government laws and church doctrines, the tape of family expectations, and the tape of needing one another to face life's uncertainties. With all that tape wrapped around the box, it took a mighty explosion from inside for it to come apart. People stayed married even when they experienced no happiness or personal fulfillment from the marriage.

One by one the tapes have been cut. This means that few external forces keep couples together if the glue of commitment and love dries up and flakes off. Even when this glue is present in the marriage, other forces can knock a marriage apart. The glue may not be enough to hold together a marriage when one partner has an affair or sets out on a new career that threatens the other in some way. It may not be strong enough to hold through crises such as unemployment, or serious long-term illness, or the death of a child. Because of this, marriages in America are much less sturdy than they were in the past.

Rapid Changes Offer More Choices

Rapid changes in our society offer many more choices about how to live our lives. In the past, what was expected of persons when they married was fairly well established. Boys learned from their fathers how to be husbands, and girls learned from their mothers how to be wives. Young people prepared for marriage by preparing to fill a certain role in adult life. A symbol of this was the "hope chest" that a young woman began preparing in the hope of marrying. She put in it hand-embroidered household linens and other such items that she would need to be a proper wife. Whether she would marry Joshua Graham or Benjamin Smith did not affect how she prepared for marriage. Young men, on the other hand, needed to establish themselves in a business or on a farm and prove themselves stable and able to support a wife.

Young people today prepare for marriage in quite different ways. They focus on the person they will marry and their relationship with them. They ask themselves such questions as: Are we compatible? Do we have the same values? Do we love one another enough? They do not prepare for a role—"husband" or "wife"—but instead examine the relationship with a specific person and decide if this person is *the one*. A young woman thinks that the most important question is whether she loves Josh Graham or Ben Smith, not whether she is prepared to be a wife or even if he is prepared to be a husband. We tend not to think about marriage as a role we take on. It is instead a decision one makes based on feelings about a specific person.

The young woman with the hope chest a hundred years ago probably would have lived a very similar life no matter which man in her community she might have married. If she lived in rural America, her days would have been filled with child care, farm chores, food preparation, gardening, and putting up produce whether as Mrs. Graham or Mrs. Smith. There were some differences, but they were small compared with the possibilities of today. When partners choose one another today, they choose not only a partner, but a life-style. Josh Graham may want to raise at least five children and live on a small farm so that he can both farm and run a small business in town. Ben Smith may want to have no children and live in a town house in a large city where he and his wife can develop their careers and travel overseas frequently. The differences can multiply.

We want to marry a person whose dreams fit our own. We do not just want a spouse who can support us as best as can be expected. We want one whose values and goals in life mesh with ours. If we find such a person, the marriage seems made in heaven. We live, however, in a world in which rapid change is the rule. For example, many persons now have two or even three careers in a lifetime. We move from place to place following our jobs or our dreams. Our personal dreams and values change over time, and the dreams that brought us together may be discarded five years into marriage. A young couple may share a dream of living and serving in the inner city. Several years later, however, one longs to have children and live in a home with a yard and a neighborhood where the kids can safely ride their bicycles. The other feels that to make such a move would be abandoning everything for which they had worked. When values and dreams do not appear to fit together anymore, the marriage faces a crisis.

People Live Longer

Marriages can last for many years, as people live longer. Better nutrition and medical care have lengthened the lives of Americans and, as a side product, have increased the divorce rate. Only since 1900 have people expected to live until age fifty as a couple. Before 1900 many women either died during childbirth or were widowed while they still had young children. The "empty nest," the years a husband and wife live together after their children have grown up and left home, simply did not exist (Skolnick & Skolnick, 1980).

When life was shorter, a vow to live with a partner until death was not as long a commitment as it is today. If a husband did not die, he might expect to go through several wives because of the high death rate for women in childbirth. Today, we may live together thirty years or more after the youngest child leaves home. Marriages that last half a century or more are not worth news coverage today because they are so common. As Jessie Bernard has observed, "Nowadays, people have a much longer time in which to discover how unhappy their marriages are" (Bernard, 1982, p. 98).

The Bright Side of the News About American Marriages

When we look at the changes in marriage today, we can see some silver linings in the ominous clouds of rising divorce rates. Americans believe in marriage and expect much from it. Our society no longer forces people to stay in painful, crippling marriages; spouses are free to choose to stay together or leave one another, just as they were free to marry in the first place. Partners have many more options about how to shape their marriages to fit their dreams and values, which for Christians involves their understanding of God's calling in service as individuals and as a couple. And, finally, when couples commit themselves to love one another faithfully "until death do us part," they are committing themselves to a long, long life together.

It is hard to see the silver lining in a cloud, however, when you are getting drenched in a thunderstorm. Many couples in our society are indeed in the middle of marital storms. Their marriages do not live up to their expectations. They feel lonely and hurt in a relationship that was supposed to offer companionship and comfort. Since the only thing that is supposed to hold marriage together in our culture is the love and commitment of the partners, they look at their feelings of anger and frustration with one another and wonder why they should stay together when their marriage seems so empty. They cannot seem to change how they feel. They are unhappy and feel stuck, but they are not sure that divorce is an answer either. They look at the many possibilities in life that they see on television or in the lives of people they know and imagine how different, and, they assume, how much better, their life might be. Then they picture their marriage twenty years from now if it keeps on the way it is presently. It does not measure up to their dreams, or to what society promotes as a good marriage.

Christian Faith and Marriage Problems

This book is written for Christians struggling with questions about their marriage or who want to understand the struggles of others they know and love whose marriages are troubled. As most of us know, Christians have marriage problems, too. We live in this world and are children of this land and this age. All of these changes and stresses on marriage sound familiar to us, because we live with them, too. In addition, Christians expect to live out their faith with their marital partners according to God's will; and this sometimes seems to be a tall order.

In the Bible, marriage is often used to picture God's relationship with the people with whom God has made a covenant. In the Old Testament, for example, Hosea's relationship with his wife Gomer was intended to be an illustration for Israel of God's steadfast love even when the Israelites kept turning away from God in sin. As a living picture of God's love and desire to redeem Israel, Hosea took Gomer, a common prostitute, and married her (Hos. 1:2). Gomer bore three children, and all three were assumed not to be the children of Hosea. To no one's surprise, she then deserted him and the kids. Yet Hosea, against all common sense, went after her to bring her home again (3:1-5).

The lesson the prophet taught was about God's steadfast love for Israel even when Israel had cheated on God and chased after other gods. God will not give up on Israel but will love her back to decency. What is interesting for us is that this is one of many images of struggling marriages used in the Old Testament to describe Israel's relationship with God (see also Jer. 2:2, 3:1,6-8; Ezek. 16:8-32; Hos. 2:7-8,19-20). We can assume, then, that in the days of the prophets, people were all too familiar with marriage troubles.

In the New Testament, marriage is used to picture God's love for the church through Christ. The church is identified as the Bride of Christ (Rev. 21:9). In Ephesians 5:21-33, Paul used how "Christ loved the church and gave himself up for her" (v. 25) as an illustration of how married partners are to love one another. Here the quality of the relationship between husband and wife takes center stage. More is expected of married partners than just to stay faithful to one another. They are to show in their relationship with one another the self-giving love of Christ for the church. Marriage is not just living happily ever after in starry-eyed bliss; the love of husband and wife for one another is to mirror Christ's sacrificial love.

Jesus' command to love our neighbor as ourself applies to the person who sleeps next to us just as much as it does to the people who live in our neighborhood and in distant places. But loving our marriage partner may be a greater challenge. Love is to be a witness to the world of our faith: "By this all men will know that you are my disciples, if you have love for one another" (John 13:35). It is not as hard to go the occasional extra mile for a friend, and perhaps even for a stranger. That may happen only once in a while. Marriage requires that we go the extra mile for our partner every day. And it is often required at times when we are already exhausted from the pushes and pulls of the world beyond our marriage.

Marriage is a hard test for our Christian love. We must put up with our partner's irritating habits, make all our decisions keeping in mind the effects on our partner, and adjust our most private dreams to fit with those of our partner. When we marry, we make the decision to give our very life to one another. From that moment on, our lives are forever altered. The troubles we experience may be a sign of our failure, but our struggle to overcome them with love and commitment is a sign not only of our faith in marriage, but even more, our faith in God and the way of Christ.

Not All Marriage Troubles Are the Same

When we have troubles in our family or marriage, we often feel very alone. No one else seems to have troubles quite like ours. In some sense this is true; every marriage is unique. The problems that we face in our lives together mirror who we are as a couple. In some ways we are different from every other couple. Yet we also share experiences that are common in many marriages.

Marriage troubles are rooted in one or more of three different levels in a marriage: within one partner, between partners, and in the world surrounding the marriage. These troubles can be compared to different kinds of illnesses. *Troubles within one partner* are like a disorder or disease in one body system, such as cancer in the lung or stones in the kidney. *Troubles between partners* are like a problem in the way body systems relate to one another. There are too many teeth to fit the jaw structure, or the jaws are not aligned with one another correctly, requiring surgery to bring them into line. Finally, *troubles in the world around the marriage* are like diseases caused by poor nutrition or exposure to deadly chemicals or radiation. Although all three kinds of disorders result in pain and suffering, doing something about the trouble requires knowing what is causing it.

Problems One Partner Faces

In marriage, the two are to become one. Does this mean that people are not whole until they marry? Or are people whole until they marry, and then they shrink into halves that cannot exist without each other? We often hear someone talk about the marriage partner as "my better half."

Jesus made it clear that we each are whole persons. In 1 Corinthians 12:27, Paul said that we are *individually* members of the body of Christ. We are created, called, and redeemed as individuals. Even though we become part of the one-flesh unity of marriage, we remain whole persons. We will be resurrected as individuals, not as marriage partners (see Matt. 22:23-32). Marriage is not a part of the next life. Therefore, we do not become whole by getting married. Wholeness comes through our relationship with God, not with a marriage partner.

Although a marriage partner can offer companionship, comfort, and love, in the end we still face life alone with our own thoughts and doubts. Many of the troubles and joys which come to us in life come to us first as individuals. These personal troubles and joys, however, can have a big impact on our marriage. Struggling with alcohol, drug, or food addictions affects our marriage. Personal struggles with depression, anxiety, and difficulty with making decisions create stress and trouble in a marriage. We come to marriage not as a lump of clay to be molded by the marriage, but with personality characteristics, strengths, and weaknesses already formed that will influence the characteristics, strengths, and weaknesses of our marriage.

It is not only what we bring to the marriage as individuals, but also the personal changes we experience throughout our lives which affect our marriage. We change physically; every breath brings change as we breathe out that which has been a part of us and bring in that which is new. Look at your wedding pictures; if you have been married more than five years, there is not a single atom in your body that was a part of you when you married (Lemley, 1986). We are constantly changing physically. The physical changes we go through are only a symbol of the many changes that we experience that have an impact on marriage. Our *health changes*. One partner struggles with a life-threatening illness, or a chronic condition such as arthritis or heart disease, which places severe limits on life. Another partner may lose fifty pounds and feel more attractive and energetic, or may gain fifty pounds and feel unattractive and depressed. We go through *developmental changes*. Pregnancy and the birth of children, mid-life crises, an empty nest, menopause, and diminishing physical strength all have a profound impact on us as individuals and, therefore, on marriage. Finally, *environmental changes* occur. A best friend moves away. We get a new boss who does not like us. Or we find ourselves in the midst of a crisis at church. Simply joining a softball team may have an impact on our marriage.

Not all of these changes create troubles in marriage, of course. How they affect our marriage depends on our relationship. Joining a softball team may cause resentment or conflict in marriage if the partner does not want you to be gone from home several evenings a week for practice and games. Or it may create more enjoyment in the marriage if the partner likes going with you and cheering for you, or looks forward to some quiet time at home alone while you are gone. In the same way, illness may create strain in a marriage that leads to conflict and distance between partners, or it may pull partners together as they see with new eyes how much they cherish one another. In chapter 2 we will look at what we can do when individual problems create marital troubles.

Problems Between Partners

Many times the changes or problems that one of us experiences as an individual lead to marital trouble because they point out how different we are. No partner agrees about everything or sees life in exactly the same way as the other partner. If they did, how boring life would be! Our differences are the source of the growth and change we experience as persons and as a couple. One spouse is very neat and orderly; the other spouse is messy and loves to do things on the spur of the moment. Both can learn from the other's traits, and each may value what the other brings to the marriage. The neat, orderly partner needs the messy, spur-of-the-moment one, who can ignore chores for the moment to take time to go for a picnic or take a walk in the first snow of the year. The messy, spur-of-the-moment one needs the order and organization that the other can bring to what may otherwise be a life of chaos.

We can see that these same differences that help bring balance to our lives can also create conflict and trouble. The neat, orderly one wants to save a portion of the income each month for some future goal; the messy, spur-of-the-moment one wants to worry about the future tomorrow and take the extra money to buy a sailboat or a new stereo. We have to come to some agreement on a whole array of issues such as money, work, household chores and maintenance, sexual and emotional intimacy, children, in-laws, friends, church and our faith, how to spend our spare time, and how to plan for the future. Different ways of seeing things and doing things can lead to trouble.

The way we relate to one another can also create trouble. For example, partners may be in a power struggle in which every issue becomes a battle to see who can be king or queen of the mountain. Or, both partners may want the other to be in control, so that whatever happens, they will not have to feel responsible. We see this played out in the little spat over where to go out to eat: "I don't care, dear; it's up to you." One of the hidden messages may be, "You decide, and that way, if the service is bad or the food is not very good, or the bill is too high, it will be your fault."

Chapter 3 will examine how we can go about making changes in the patterns that develop in our marriage. Since the need for change, as well as the changes themselves, often create anger and conflict, Chapter 4 will look at how Christians can constructively handle conflict and anger in marriage. One area of married life which is particularly sensitive and difficult to change is our sexual relationship. Chapter 5 will explore the role of sexuality in the lives of married Christians and the ways we can make changes in our sexual life together.

Problems from the World Around the Marriage

The world in which a couple finds themselves living can also create troubles for a marriage. The environment of a marriage includes the *physical context* in which the couple lives (a burst water pipe that ruins the floors and walls, a refrigerator that stops working, heat and humidity that make partners grumpy and miserable). It also includes the *interpersonal context* (a baby that cries from 2 AM until 4 AM every night, a widowed mother who is seriously ill and needs to be either moved into the home or into a nursing facility, an employer who insists that one partner work more overtime). Finally, the environment includes the *context of cultural ideas and beliefs*. The

marriages of friends and neighbors and the notions couples get
about marriage from newspapers, television shows, and magazines may be quite different from their own marriage. These
give couples different perspectives to look at their own lives
together and how they might make changes (things to buy to
make life more comfortable and enjoyable, how their marriage
can be more satisfying, how to discipline their children, what
the "best" ways to do things are). Sometimes these new ideas
are helpful. Sometimes they may make us feel even more unhappy and frustrated with the ways our own marriage fail to
measure up.

Many of the troubles spouses struggle with involve all three
contexts of their environment. In deciding what to do with
their ill mother, for example, a couple not only has to consider
their relationship with her and whether or not having her
move into their home is what she and they want *(the interpersonal context)* but also their *physical context*. Do they have
space? Does their home have too many stairs? Can they afford
in-home nursing care? They also may be dealing with what
society expects in such a situation, that is, what we referred to
as the *context of cultural ideas and beliefs*. Will people think
we are unloving to put her in a nursing home? Will she be
happier there because most aging parents do not want to burden their children? Will it create marriage problems for us if
she lives here with us?

In chapter 6, we will look at ways we can cope with strains
that come from the world around us. We will give special attention to the troubles in a marriage that are rooted in relationships with parents and other family members, work, children,
and money. We will also explore the purpose of marriage not
only in the lives of the two partners, but also in the world in
which they find themselves.

In summary, troubles in a marriage can arise not only from

the grinding of gears that happens when two different people try to mesh their values and patterns of living together. They can also begin when one partner struggles with personal troubles, or when the marriage is bombarded by demands from the surrounding world.

Problems can also begin at one level and then spread to involve one or both of the other levels. Like a disease spreading throughout the body, the problems of one partner can overwhelm a marriage. Problems with the world around us, such as conflict with in-laws or troubles at work, often create tension and trouble between partners and heighten anxiety and trouble in one or both as individuals.

Every marriage has troubles. From the beginning of the honeymoon until one partner is in the grave, partners struggle with their weaknesses, their differences, and with the crises that life brings their way. Although all marriages have troubles, not all marriages are "in trouble." Underneath the storms in some marriages, partners feel the sturdiness of a solid rock of love and commitment. Marriages in trouble, however, have their very foundations shaken by the conflict or crisis with which partners are struggling. They need help not only in dealing with the particular storm, but also in assessing damage to the foundation of their relationship and making repairs. What are some of the signs of a marriage "in trouble?"

Warning Signs of a Troubled Marriage

We Keep Secrets About Our Marriage From One Another
All partners keep secrets from one another. We do not share our every thought, every dream, every feeling with our partner. If we did, we would probably bore one another to death! We make choices about what we want to share and what we want to keep to ourselves. We are very complicated creatures,

and it would be impossible to tell our partners everything we thought and felt even if that is what we wanted to do. Our private thoughts, feelings, and dreams serve as a well of resources from which we draw to keep our marriage interesting, growing, and changing.

Keeping secrets that are important to the marriage, on the other hand, is a sign of trouble. Susan served as "best-supporting actress" for her husband Mark's business career for eighteen years. She entertained his business friends, took most of the responsibility for the children, and cared for their home. Several times she said to him how much she wished that she had finished college, but Mark pooh-poohed her wish, saying, "What's the point? I make plenty of money and you'll never need to work. I like you just the way you are." Susan privately determined, however, that when the children left home, that was just exactly what she would do, regardless of what Mark said. When her youngest child left for college, Susan enrolled, too. When she announced to Mark what she had done, he responded, "There is no way my wife is going to do any such thing!" Susan's response was, "Fine! I'll see a lawyer tomorrow!"

Mark and Susan faced a change much like the changes that all couples experience at times in their marriage. Throughout our lives together, we struggle to fit together when we are both changing and the world around us is changing, too. Susan wanted to be home when her children were babies, but she felt restless and that her life did not mean much when the babies became teenagers that were home only a few hours of the day. She was ready for a change. The problem was that she kept secret her need for a personal change that would also affect her marriage. When Mark was not happy about her desire to go back to school, she said no more about it. She did not tell Mark how important this was to her. He helped her to keep the secret by not listening to what she did say. He cut off her several attempts to tell him. Instead of working through her desire for change together and facing their conflict, they took the easy route. They said nothing. They made their decisions alone; and, consequently, they grew apart. Susan made her plans alone, and Mark kept his eyes and ears closed to her needs. Quietly, she became more angry, resentful, and determined. He became more blind and deaf to the changing climate in their marriage.

We may not share every thought and feeling about our marriage and our partner with one another. But when thoughts or feelings come again and again, it is time to talk.

We Focus on the Flaws in Our Marriage, Not the Beautiful Parts

Every marriage has problems. Having problems does not mean our marriage is in trouble. There are times when we argue over trivial issues, or when we think our partner acts like a boob, or when we cannot agree about something that is important to each of us. When we focus on the troubled parts of our relationship, we cannot see the parts of the marriage that are running smoothly. It is like stubbing your toe. For the moment, all you can think about is your toe and how much it hurts. It is hard to reflect on how good your ears or your fingers feel.

Sometimes a marriage suffers from something like "new-car fever." Many of us have experienced wanting to buy a new car. Suddenly, your old car looks like a piece of junk. Every dent and spot of rust glares at you. It seems noisy and sluggish. All of its problems stick out. The brake job it needs will cost an astronomical sum for a car you now think is on its last legs. The same car a month before, however, may have seemed quite all right to you, even though it has hardly changed at all. What has changed is *you*. You look at it differently now. When we are making a decision, we tend to color everything in favor of the decision we are about to make. It makes you feel better to spend all that money if your old car looks like a pile of junk to you.

When we find ourselves focusing on all the flaws in our marriage, then, it may be a sign that we are making a decision. We are saying to ourselves, "This marriage is really a pile of junk. It's time to trade it in for something else." We may not have even allowed ourselves to think that particular thought yet, but our evaluation of the relationship as mostly bad or as a mistake is the first step to ending it.

We tell friends and others we trust about our partner's flaws or our marriage problems.—Just like every marriage has problems, every spouse confides in a friend on occasion about something the spouse has done. Women talk about men and men talk about women. Usually such talk is not aimed at shooting our partners in the back. We tell a story about our partner's forgetfulness or grumpiness, and it is usually told with a tone of loving tolerance. It is probably not a story our partner would especially mind being told. He or she admits to being forgetful or grumpy in the morning.

On the other hand, when we find ourselves telling a friend how miserable our marriage is, or how we dislike our partner's ways, it is a sign of trouble. We have not only told ourselves our marriage is a pile of junk; now we are "going public" with our opinion. When we have told others who are important to us how bad things are, we almost feel embarrassed not to do something about it. If there seems nothing else to do, that "something" may be pulling out of the marriage.

We keep fighting about the same thing over and over, yet nothing ever changes.—Susan and Mark talked several times about her going back to school. Each time, however, sounded like a tape recording of the time before. They were not able to make any progress in their arguments. Each time the distance between them increased until finally they did not talk about it at all. The wedge of misunderstanding and conflict split them apart, first emotionally and spiritually, and, finally, physically. A couple may continue to live together; but, because anger and distance poisons their relationship, they are guilty of breaking their marriage vows to love and cherish just as the couple who divorces.

In every marriage, some of the same issues come up again and again. A neat spouse and a messy spouse may squabble over and over about keeping clothes picked up. In a good marriage, however, partners reach some compromise over time. Perhaps they still argue about being too neat and being too messy, but now they argue about wiping off the kitchen counter, or where the messy one can and cannot pile personal belongings. Over time, some changes are made and the conflict moves to other issues. In a troubled marriage, by contrast, the partners seem to spin their wheels and get stuck deeper and deeper in the mire. They may give up trying to resolve their conflict altogether. Nothing seems to change, and both become more and more certain that things will never change.

We do not love one another anymore.—Too often, this becomes an announcement that a marriage has died. To be sure, the absence of loving feelings for one another is a serious warning sign. But to say that the marriage is dead because we do not feel love for one another is like a doctor looking at a man unconscious from an electrical shock and proclaiming that he is dead because he is not breathing. If the doctor can find a pulse, there may still be life; and breathing can be restored.

The truth is that feelings come and go. Times come in every marriage when we no longer want to be with one another all the time, when the partner's ways are no longer endearing but a pain in the neck, and when we do not feel overcome with joy each time our partner speaks. In a troubled marriage, those scattered clouds of anger, irritation, and boredom begin to mount up until we no longer feel any love at all. When this happens, it is like the red lights on the dashboard of a car; these feelings flash a warning sign to us that there is serious trouble. Few of us, however, sell our cars because we need gas or oil or because the engine has overheated. We get the fuel or repairs we need, and we do it quickly before we become stranded in a broken-down car.

God's feelings with Israel were often anger and frustration (such as in Num. 11:1,10). God did not ignore these feelings, nor did God abandon Israel as a hopelessly stiff-necked people and try out a new group. God remained faithful to the covenant and told Israel in no uncertain terms about the need for change (vv. 16-25). The covenant between God and Israel, and the covenant between a husband and wife, is not the result only of loving feelings, but also of the decision to act faithfully. The insistence, "We just don't love one another anymore," is not a valid reason for Christians to abandon their marriage. But neither is it a crisis that can be ignored. Instead, partners ought to sound an alarm that change is needed. We have committed ourselves to one another in spite of any negative feelings, and we are to live out that commitment by tackling the sources of these feelings.

Our marriage is held together by only one of the partners.— Marriages are covenant relationships, and it takes two persons to make and keep a covenant. It was not enough for God to love and claim Israel; Israel also had to recognize Yahweh as her God. It is not enough for God to love us through the death and resurrection of Jesus Christ; we must claim the promises offered to us and commit ourselves to a life lived in relationship with God. Covenants cannot be one-sided.

The Bible is full of examples of one partner in a covenant straying. Over and over, Israel strayed after other gods; and God called them back. In marriage, too, times come when one partner carries the weight of the marriage. We remain faithful when our partner is not; we try when the partner has stopped trying. The commitment of just one partner cannot keep a marriage alive if no restoration comes, however.

Our marriage has always been like this; we cannot change now.—We discussed earlier the levels of marital problems. Changes and demands on the marriage come from both within each of the partners as well as from the world outside the marriage. When the marriage can stand up to these changes or can adapt to fit new demands, it remains strong. When partners plant their feet and refuse to change, however, the marriage is in trouble. Mark stated that he would not change to fit Susan's desire to return to school. "Our marriage has always worked with me working and you at home; and I'm not about to change now." Susan believed him; nothing in the marriage will ever change. That did not end her own dreams, however; what ended was her hope for her marriage.

It is good to struggle with and take our time in making changes in our marriages. If we did not, our marriages would be as changeable as the weather. We need to have the security of knowing what to expect from one another most of the time. Our marriage, after all, is the safe "home base" in what sometimes looks like a frantic game of tag in the workaday world. Yet every couple has to change their pattern of living over time. The young couple who starts out by doing everything together—the shopping, the laundry, the housecleaning—finds that pattern no longer works when they have two small children. Now they need to split up the work to get it all done. They can no longer take time to decide carefully and be sure that they agree about which cut of meat to buy for supper. Now one shops while the other cares for children; one pays the bills while the other washes dishes.

The couple which cannot or will not change would be fine if neither person changed and the world around them stayed the same. But we change with every breath we take.

If one or more of these warning signs are present in a marriage, it is time to do a serious check up to find out both the source of the troubles as well as the damage to the relationship that needs to be repaired. It is hoped that this book will be helpful in this check up. In chapter 7, we will look at the need for forgiveness and repentance as first steps in making changes in marriage. It may be that a couple experiencing trouble can do a marriage audit and make needed adjustments on their own. Others may need the help of someone they trust to counsel and guide them through this process—a professional counselor. Members of a church staff, a family and children's agency, or a community mental health center are often helpful in identifying someone qualified to offer such help.

For some couples, divorce seems to be the best path out of a painful marriage that is destroying both partners as individuals. In chapter 8, we will look at what the Bible says about divorce and how Christians can make decisions about and live through and beyond a divorce.

2

What Can We Do When One Partner's Problems Threaten Our Marriage?

As we discussed in chapter 1, marital troubles are not all the result of poor communication, or conflict over roles, or power struggles. Some problems arise because of who we are as individuals when we enter the marriage and the changes we go through as individuals during our life together. Because we try to mesh our lives together—we become "one flesh" (Gen. 2:24)—our personal quirks and problems cannot help but affect the marriage relationship. In this chapter, we will discuss some of the personal problems which can affect a marriage.

Identifying Personal Problems

Marriage Does Not Meet Our Expectations

In chapter 1, we talked about the great expectations that many Americans bring to marriage. Before the wedding bells ring, the engaged partners may think to themselves, *At last I have found someone who will keep me from ever feeling lonely again; who will understand me and love me no matter what; who will always be attractive and sexy and find me to be so, too; who will share my hopes and dreams; who will need me and want to be with me;* and so on. They anticipate that this one they love will make them whole and will be strong where they are weak.

Sarah was the oldest of six children. Her father was an alcoholic, and her parents were often separated. Her mother worked long, hard hours to support her children. Much of the care of her younger brothers and sisters fell to Sarah. Despite the load of chores at home, Sarah was an excellent student and enjoyed an active social life. She was determined not to marry a man like her father. She wanted someone who would be dependable and would take care of her. She fell in love with and married Tom. He was tall and big, and she felt safe snuggled under his arm. She loved the way he took charge and made decisions. He told her, "I don't want you to worry your pretty little head about anything. I just want you to love me and be there for me."

Early in the marriage, Sarah enjoyed her new freedom from responsibility. Tom made all the decisions. He paid the bills and gave her an allowance. She had no idea how much money he made; she just knew it was enough for them to live well. After awhile, however, Sarah began to feel frustrated and out of control of her own life. She began to worry that Tom might not make the "right" decisions, namely, the decisions that she would make. She began to realize that she wanted a husband that she could depend on, but not one that would treat her like a helpless child. She also began to notice that he was deeply worried about something; but he kept it to himself, saying he was handling things. One day while he was at work, a bill collector called, asking why they had not made their last three mortgage payments. Sarah was first shocked and then felt betrayed. Tom was no different from her father! He had let her down in the one thing she counted on the most from him— security. As a result, the foundation of her commitment to Tom was shaken.

We need to look carefully at our feelings that our marriage is not measuring up to our expectations, when we begin to say to ourselves, *I expect to get certain things out of this marriage that I'm not getting*. The focus is on what we can "get out of" marriage. We are asking, "What is in it for me?" For Christians, this means that we have things backwards. Nowhere in the Bible does it say that relationships are to meet our needs or that we should get out of them what we want or even need. Christians are to have their lives directed toward giving, not getting. The basic principle of Christian living is self-giving. Jesus said, "For whoever would save his life will lose it, and whoever loses his life for my sake will find it" (Matt. 16:25; see also Matt. 10:39; Mark 8:35; Luke 9:24; 17:33; and John 12:25). In a marriage relationship, this means that if we base our commitment to our partner on whether or not we are getting what we think we want or need from the marriage, we are on shaky ground. In the end, we will lose.

Helmut Thielicke wrote about a very old couple who seemed to radiate happiness. He was particularly taken with the wife, who, in spite of the fact that she was crippled and ill, still showed gratitude for life. As he grew to know them, he learned that her husband dearly loved her, "and it was as if she were like a stone that has been lying in the sun for years and years, absorbing its radiant warmth, and now was reflecting back cheerfulness and warmth and serenity" (Thielicke, 1961, p. 99). It was not because she had been such a wonderful, radiant person that she was loved so much by her husband. Instead, it was because she had been loved so much that she had become the person she now was. The question for us as spouses is not, "Have I married the right person?" Instead, we need to turn this around: "Have I loved my partner too little, that I have caused him or her to become cold, or critical, or boring?" According to Thielicke, "the other person, whom God has joined to me, is never what he is apart from me. *He is not only bone of my bone; he is also boredom of my boredom and lovelessness of my lovelessness*" (Thielicke, 1961, p. 100).

What do we do, then, when we feel betrayed, as Sarah did, or frustrated because the marriage is not meeting our needs in some way? First, we must recognize that the problem must be addressed by me. We should say to ourselves, "I have a need that is not being met," not "This marriage is awful because it doesn't do for me what it is supposed to do." We also need to ask ourselves, "What have I done to create or contribute to the problem?" It would be easy for Sarah to decide that her marriage was a mistake. She could bitterly complain, "You're untrustworthy just like Daddy. I can't believe I let myself be fooled into marrying someone like you." This may be exactly how she feels. But she and Tom can better deal with the crisis of trust in their relationship if she can say to herself and to Tom, "I thought I wanted to be taken care of, for you to be my guardian angel. But I'm not willing to live with the results of your making all the decisions. I want to be able to depend on you, but, at the same time, I want to have a say in what's happening. I want to share the burdens with you and not let you shoulder them alone." If she does this, she does not pass judgment on the marriage, but she takes responsibility for her part in it.

We Face Temptations

As human beings we have freedom, but with freedom comes temptation. Jesus could not have been truly tempted in the wilderness had He not been free to choose a different path for His life (Matt. 4:1-11). He chose to reject the devil's enticements and confirm His calling to give His life as a sacrifice for many (20:28). In marriage, we choose whether or not to live faithfully with our partner. We do not finish with the decision about marriage when we say "I do" at the altar. Each day, over and over, we decide whether we will live faithfully to our commitment. Each day, we face temptations that could pull us away from our covenant.

The temptations that come in marriage are similar to the

temptations we face in our relationship with God. As Christians, we are tempted to go after false gods and commit to them because we mistakenly believe that they can better supply us with what we want. In our marriage relationship, we are also tempted *to be unfaithful*. We may find ourselves tempted to go after other partners, someone who looks to us to be better than our spouse. We do not have to have sexual relations with another to have been unfaithful. An affair is just the end result of a secret search for another to replace the spouse. We think that this one can give us something our spouse has been unable to give.

We are also tempted in our Christian lives to accept cheap grace. We want to receive all the benefits of salvation without living a faithful life. Works are not the root of faith, but both James (Jas. 2:14-22) and Paul (Gal. 5:6) agree that they are the fruit of faith. So James argues, "Faith by itself, if it has no works, is dead" (Jas. 2:17; see Matt. 7:21-27). True faith leads to fruitful service for God. In the same way that we are tempted to take God's offer of salvation for granted, we are tempted *to take our partner's love for granted*. We assume that our partner loves us and is committed to us but do nothing to nurture the relationship between us. We may even convince ourselves that our partner owes us love and faithfulness. This attitude will lead to trouble. The commitment we have to one another may be freely chosen, but we must work to nurture and strengthen that commitment throughout our lives.

On the other hand, Christians are also tempted to try to earn their way into good standing. We may fool ourselves into thinking that if we just live "good" lives, not hurting anyone else and doing good deeds, God is bound to save us. We begin to act like the Pharisee in Jesus' parable who came to the Temple to worship as if it were Show and Tell—he paraded before God and others all of his good deeds and expected to receive a gold star. We forget that we are actually like the tax collector who could boast of nothing but only beat his breast and plead, "God, be merciful to me, a sinner!" (Luke 18:9-14). We cannot come to God able to boast of our righteous achievements. We can only come to God as sinners who must confess that we are unworthy servants (17:9-10) and lucky to be still in God's employ.

As spouses, we may have difficulty discounting our worthiness and *admitting our failings* to one another. We frequently would like to tell our partner, "I work so hard, I do so many things for you, I have made so many sacrifices, how can you possibly be angry with me for one little thing? In fact, you owe me for all that I have done for you!" We have trouble admitting to ourselves and to our partner our need for forgiveness. Sometimes we blame our partner for all the problems and refuse to see our own part in the trouble we face.

Finally, Christians are sometimes tempted to treat God like an Aladdin's lamp, a means to get our every wish. Sometimes our prayers can be little different from making a wish and blowing out birthday candles. Jesus warned us not to pray like pagans whose prayers reflect their assumption that the wheel that squeaks gets the grease. They heap up empty phrases thinking "that they will be heard for their many words" (Matt. 6:7). Their prayers are meant only to manipulate God to their own advantage. Jesus taught us to pray not to bend God's will but to lay hold of God's willingness to bless us. Jesus taught us to ask God for what we need, but our asking is to be in the context of a personal relationship of love and worship (v. 8). We are not to try to manipulate God for our own purposes but to open ourselves to God so that God's purposes might be done (vv. 9-10).

Spouses are tempted to *treat one another like objects to be used*. We try to force or manipulate the other person to be or do or think certain ways. For example, a wife wants her husband to spend more time with her talking about things and less time watching the Cubs games on TV. Telling him what she wants does not seem to bring about any change, so she becomes coldly silent whenever the television is turned on. On evenings that the television is off, on the other hand, she makes a point to be loving and attentive to her husband. By doing so, she hopes to get him to watch television less. Instead of working out their differences together, she is trying to manipulate the change the way she wants it to go. She is treating her husband like an object, a thing she can mold and shape to fit her needs.

No marriage is perfect, and we go through times when we want our partner to make changes. There is nothing wrong with asking for what we need or want from our spouse. But trying to force or manipulate our partner to change not only will eventually backfire on us but will also turn our marriage into a power game to see who can control the other. Our submission to one another is to be freely given, not coerced (Eph. 5:21).

Our Values Change

We mentioned in chapter 1 the many changes that partners go through in their lifetimes. We may begin marriage with the same values and dreams, but each of us changes over the course of time. Sometimes we change in different ways.

Paul addressed this problem in instructions to those who had become Christians and were married to non-Christians. They had radically changed their values. As a result, some worried that, as a part of the body of Christ, they were being defiled by their continuing marriage to a pagan (1 Cor. 7:12-13). They thought that, because of the change that had taken place in them as a result of their new commitment to Christ, they should divorce their unbelieving spouses. Partners whose values had changed dramatically through their conversion soon found out that their new values and life goals were at odds with those of their partners. Paul told them that this was not grounds for divorce. They were not defiled by marriage to a pagan. Quite the contrary, as Christians, they sanctified their partners. Therefore, he told them not to split the marriage unless the unbelieving partner absolutely insisted (vv. 14-16). Paul recommended that they stay married in spite of the difficulties they would encounter because of their faith commitment.

Often, when our values change, we feel we have "nothing in common" anymore. What may have seemed so important to us when we married loses its influence on our lives. Jane and Adam married right after high school graduation. Both were determined to have more in life than their parents, working-class people who had scrimped and saved for everything they had. Adam and Jane both worked part time and lived very simply while they attended college, majoring in business. They dreamed of the day when they could own their own home, take luxury vacations, and eat out without having to use coupons or trade in pop bottles to have enough money. The first years after they finished college were filled with buying things—a home, furniture, a new car, nice clothes.

Fifteen years later, however, Adam felt unsatisfied. The beautiful home with the lovely furniture did not bring him contentment. Their life together seemed for him to hold little meaning or purpose. He wanted to do something that would make him feel that his life had counted for something. He dreamed of and began to talk about going back to school to study forestry and working for a wilderness preservation group. Jane was devastated by Adam's dream. She loved their city life, and she saw everything they had worked so hard to get and that she loved so much being lost. Yet Adam was restless and unhappy. They must either come to a parting of the ways or somehow come to terms with their now different values.

Our values do not always shift so dramatically. We do, however, go through changes in what we consider important to us, changes that may not fit the contract we have developed with one another about how we will live our lives together. Unless partners can face these changes together and find ways to meet the concerns of both partners—in other words, to learn to live with their differences—the marriage faces serious trouble.

Our Marriage Requires More Than We Can Give

Sometimes we simply do not have the energy and resources to give the love, support, and sharing of ourselves that marriage requires. In many ways, this is the flip side of the first problem we talked about—marriage not measuring up to our expectations. In this case, we do not have what it takes to measure up to the expectations of our partner. Perhaps we struggle with a chronic physical illness that drains us of energy and keeps us focused on our own pain or limitation so that we have little to give to our partner. Perhaps we have become addicted to alcohol or work so that everything else in our life—including our partner—gets little attention. It may be that emotional problems limit what we can give in marriage. Perhaps we have difficulty telling anyone, even our spouse, what we think or feel. Perhaps depression and anxiety overwhelm us; or painful childhood experiences make it difficult for us to like ourselves or trust someone of the opposite sex, including our partner.

These, like all the other problems we have discussed, can create trouble in a marriage. Possibly the hardest of all is admitting that we have the problem in the first place, and that, try as we might, we have failed to overcome or cope well with it. Admitting to ourselves and to our partner that we have a personal problem is the big first step in facing the problem together.

Facing Personal Problems Together

God intended the relationship between a man and a woman to keep us from having to face life alone (Gen. 2:18). When personal problems arise and spill over into marriage, we should be able to face them together. The first step in facing problems together, however, is a lonely one. We must take a good hard look at ourselves. We should:

Take Responsibility for Our Own Problems

Jesus told us in the Sermon on the Mount not to judge that we be not judged. He then drew a cartoon with words to show how silly we can look as would-be judges. He pictured someone with a two-by-four board sticking out of his eye trying to get a speck of sawdust out of the eye of another. Before he gets within three feet of the other person, he will clunk the other on the head with his two-by-four (Matt. 7:1-5). In marriage, we are often so busy pointing out the specks in our partner's eye that we do not see the huge log in our own. If we do admit to making a mistake, we often defend ourselves by implying that it was really our partner's fault. Jesus did not say that we are to ignore the faults of others. He told us to do the logging on our own eyes first before we try to help someone else. A partner rarely responds with appreciation when we reach down to them with the attitude: "You are obviously an idiot; let me show you how you are mistaken." We have to recognize how much we might also be wrong.

Let us go back for a moment to Sarah and Tom, the young woman who wanted to have a dependable husband and the young husband who wanted to protect and support her. Tom knew how important financial security was to Sarah, and he wanted badly to give it to her. When he delivered on this, he could then feel that he had been a good husband. Although his salary was enough to live on, it was not enough to allow him to give her all the things that he wanted to give her to make him feel good about himself as a husband. He began to invest money in some risky but high-yielding stocks but decided not to tell Sarah so as not to worry her. At first, he made large sums of money; and Sarah let him know how proud she was of their comfortable life together. He felt pressure to keep it up, but he began to lose money instead of making it. It all came crashing around him the day the bill collector called Sarah.

When things go sour, most of us like to have someone to blame. This has been true in marriage from the time of Adam and Eve. When Adam was caught with forbidden fruit juice stains on his tie, the first thing he did was blame Eve: "The woman whom thou gavest to be with me, she gave me fruit of the tree, and I ate" (Gen. 3:12). In this situation, Sarah blamed Tom; he handled their money poorly and tried to pretend to be more than he was in order to impress her and their friends. On the other side, Tom blamed Sarah; he felt her pressure on him to be the successful, wonderfully supportive man in her life that her father had never been. Both were sure they saw a log in their partner's eye. It is sometimes the case with us that when we stumble over our own feet we look around to see who tripped us. If something goes wrong, someone must be to blame; and, of course, it can never be me.

So who is responsible for what happened? Tom was responsible for his decision to gamble with their income. Sarah was responsible for her decision not to get involved in their money management. Marriage is a covenant in which both partners continue to be responsible for what they decide to do or not to do. When things go wrong, blaming our partners for our own decisions solves nothing and usually creates more trouble.

Recognize That Our Partners Are Responsible for Their Own Behavior

Sometimes the problem is not that we want to blame our partners for everything that goes wrong, but that we want to excuse our partner's behavior. We do not want to confront the fact that our partner has let us down or has failed in some way. We want to remain loyal and loving. Perhaps we are embarrassed by our partner's failure and hope to cover it up in some way. In these cases, we offer cheap forgiveness to keep our partner—and ourselves—from having to face up to the failure. We say things like, "It's all right; don't worry about it." "I know you didn't mean it." "It doesn't matter." "It wasn't important anyway." All the while we are saying these things, we feel deeply hurt by our partner for letting us down by breaking a promise or commitment. It is not all right, and it does matter.

God does not wink at our failures. Our sin creates a breach in our covenant with God and needs to be addressed so that the breach does not become a wide gulf separating us. Therefore, God holds us accountable. Forgiveness comes as we recognize our responsibility for what we have done, not when we try to ignore it. Marriage partners need to forgive freely; but forgiveness requires recognizing problems for what they are, not ignoring them.

Tony has been coming home hours late from work in the past few months because the work has been so heavy. At first he called his wife, Anne, when he knew he was going to be late. In the last few weeks, he has not taken the time even to do that. He used to take charge of seeing the children off to school in the morning since Anne had to be at work early. Last week he told her that he has too much to do at the office. He told her that it was up to her to rearrange her work schedule or find a sitter for the morning hours. Anne said nothing. She knows he is feeling a lot of pressure and is afraid he will explode if she confronts him about his shrinking time at home. Today, Tony announced that he has accepted a promotion that will require him to travel away from home three weeks out of each month. Anne and Tony have always made these kinds of big decisions together. Again, she says nothing, thinking to herself, *What can I do? He has already made up his mind. It will be all right. I can manage. He didn't mean to ignore my feelings; he thinks he is doing what is best for all of us. Maybe he is right. And besides, he's never home anyway.*

Anne has excused Tony's behavior. He is not responsible for hurting her; it just cannot be helped. Perhaps if Anne had talked with Tony about her feelings, he still would take the promotion. But they would have at least had a chance to talk about the way they make decisions together. Tony would be confronted with his high-handed approach that makes Anne feel like she is second fiddle to his work. She might forgive his taking her support for his decision for granted. But it would only be forgiveness if they recognized to begin with that they had a problem.

To recognize that responsibility for a problem rests in large part with me or with my partner does not mean that I should crawl off by myself to try to find my own answer. Nor may I smile smugly to myself that my partner is all to blame and think that I can therefore wash my hands of the problem. One or the other of us may be responsible for bringing the problem to the marriage, but together we are responsible for dealing with it. We share the responsibility because marriage is a covenant.

Covenants are relationships which bind two people together in lasting love, faithfulness, and devotion (Garland & Hassler, 1987). Our marriage covenant requires that we will stand by one another and help one another, no matter what. It does not mean that I will love you as long as you measure up as a partner. It means I will love you whether you measure up or not, just as God has always loved us even though we do not deserve it. It means that I will act in love, even when I do not feel very loving. It means that I will work through troubles together with you, even when I would rather escape. A covenant is "faithfulness in action" (Garland & Hassler, 1987). The model for our covenant love for one another is God's love for us. Paul wrote, "While we were yet sinners, Christ died for us" (Rom. 5:8). God did not abandon us to ourselves. As Luther said, human sin is a knot that needs God's help to undo. While we were all knotted up like a pretzel by our sin, God sent Jesus Christ to set us free and to save us. We are to live out that same kind of committed love in our covenant with our marriage partners. As we live in covenant with one another, we also bear witness to our covenant with God. Jesus said, "By this all men will know that you are my disciples, if you have love for one another" (John 13:34); and that includes love for our spouses.

We live out the promises of our covenant with one another by helping each other deal with our personal troubles and with the troubles that affect our marriage. We do this by offering one another understanding, support, and respect.

Understanding.—Letting our partners know that we understand what they are feeling and thinking and what is important to them is a powerful way of showing love. It is not easy. First, we have to *choose* to understand the other. I have to stop focusing only on what I am thinking and feeling and put myself in my partner's shoes. One of the hardest times to do that is when I feel hurt or threatened in my marriage. It is much easier to defend my own position than it is to put myself in your place and look at the problem from your eyes.

Understanding requires that we *listen*. I have to tune in to my partner's words and expressions. I have to put aside the paper or the dishes; turn off the TV, and listen. I need to stop concentrating on my own thoughts and feelings and use all my powers of understanding to figure out what is going on inside my partner.

Understanding also requires that I know myself. How do my own feelings and thoughts filter what my partner says to me? How do they keep me from knowing the parts of my partner that are different from me? What are the logs in my eye that I need to do something about before I can see, much less try to do something about, the speck in the eye of my partner?

Sometimes it is hard to show understanding for my partner because I am afraid that if I am understanding, my partner might mistake this for agreement with him. Or my partner might think that I excuse what she has done. Sarah may hesitate to say to Tom, "I know that you did what you did out of love. I understand that you were trying to do your very best." She may be afraid that Tom will respond, "That's right. So you have no right to be angry with me." But she needs to say this to him, so that he will feel understood. She also needs to help him understand her own thoughts and feelings: "I'm glad, Tom, that you feel like I understand you. But I also need you to understand me. I think I have been wrong to leave it all up to you. I want to be your partner, not your child. I want to be a part of the decisions that you make. I want them to be our decisions. I know that is different from what I have said in the past, but I want to make some changes."

Support.—We also need to let the partner know that we understand. It is not enough to have a good picture in my mind of my partner's viewpoint; I need to let her know what that picture is. When that happens, she knows whether or not she has really been understood. To know that we have been heard and understood lends comfort and support. When Sarah speaks to Tom, as she does above, he will feel supported. They still have to work through the problem together, but at least he feels that she understands him even though she may disagree with him. It is easier to hear that my partner disagrees with me if I first feel the support of being understood. It is easier to tackle problems when we both believe that we are on the same team and are not on opposing sides trying to tackle each other.

Respect.—As hard as partners may work to understand one another, understanding will not melt the differences between marriage partners. To respect one another means to accept the fact that we are different. God created us different from one another, and to respect one another means we will not try to make one another over into our own image. Respect means knowing that as much as we understand one another, we will never understand completely. Only God know us completely.

One of the ways we show our respect for one another is by recognizing that our partners know better than we do what they are thinking and feeling. That means that we do not try to tell them what they "ought" to do, or how they "ought" to feel. We are expert only on ourselves, and even then we are not always right. It is too easy to say to a spouse, "Let me tell you what you ought to do," in response to a problem the partner is experiencing. It is hard to stand by and watch someone I love, my partner, in difficulty or feeling sad or hurt. I may think that by giving my advice I am communicating love and support. I want to *do* something to make it better. It is a helpless feeling just to listen and not to take any action. No one likes feeling helpless. I think to myself, *If my partner would just do what I would do with this problem, the whole thing would be solved.* I assume that I know the situation better than my partner does.

Susan was having trouble getting over the sudden death of her mother. Months had passed since the funeral. She still found herself depressed, tired, crying frequently, and thinking all the time about how close she had been with her mother and how much she missed her. Her husband, Paul, could not stand to see her in such pain. He encouraged her to go shopping and to buy something new to wear, or to come with him to a funny movie, or to "snap out of it" by getting involved in some new activities. He finally became angry whenever she talked about her mother. He said, "If you would just listen to me, you would realize that you have got to do something with yourself! Thinking about it all the time is not helping at all!"

Susan stopped telling him about her feelings, and the tears stopped. A quiet depression settled over her, and Paul sensed she was becoming more and more distant from him. Without being able to pinpoint what was happening, he knew they were drifting apart. As much as Paul had tried to understand, he could not feel the depth of Susan's pain. He simply assumed that what worked for him when he was sad—taking his mind off things—would work for her with her grief. He wanted to help. Instead, he made her feel worse because she sensed his impatience and his wish that she were more like him.

Offering advice or trying to take charge does not respect the personhood and the responsibility of our partners for their own lives. We may help by offering suggestions, by stating what might be helpful to us if we were in our partner's place. But we should offer our own experience as a possibility for our partner, not as the final answer for what they should do.

It is a big step to come to terms with our personal responsibility—and our partner's responsibility—for some of the troubles in our marriage. Cheryl was tired from getting up several times each night with the new baby. Several evenings in a row, she exploded at David about his lack of help with all the new demands of parenthood. David snapped back that he was doing the best he could to take some of the load off her. "What more do you expect from me?" A major step forward occurred when Cheryl said, "I am tired and I feel blue. I think it's just from lack of sleep and never having a moment to myself." David then responded, "I'm tired, too, and I try to help take the load off you, but there just seems to be no end. I miss being with you when you aren't tired and tense. I try to understand, and I am sorry I get so impatient."

Both were feeling pushed from all directions. Both were facing the problem of having more required of them than they had energy to do. The result was that they blamed one another because there was no one else to blame. To confess that this was what they were doing to one another and for each to take responsibility for their actions was a major step toward resolving the difficulties.

The next step, however, turns partners back to their relationship. Even if the problem begins with each taking responsibility for themselves, a personal problem becomes a shared problem.

Find Out How the Problem Is Shaping Our Life Together

Marriages work much like our physical bodies. When there is a problem in one part, other parts adjust to make up for the problem. When arteries become clogged with cholesterol from too much fat in our diet, our heart pumps harder to circulate the blood; and our blood pressure goes up. When we are anxious, our body goes into alert, sending blood away from our digestive system and into our arms and legs so we will be ready to fight or run in response to whatever is threatening us. Often, the way our bodies try to adjust to problems in one part create other and perhaps more serious problems. High blood pressure leads to a stroke; continuing anxiety and fear lead to a variety of digestive system illnesses.

In the same way, marriage partners adjust to problems and troubles in one another. Paul responded to the depression of his wife over the death of her mother by becoming bossy, angry, and, finally, distant. Anne responded to her husband making decisions about his work that would affect the whole family without discussing them with her by becoming quiet and acting like the long-suffering, martyred wife. Jane responded to her husband's desire to change careers by feeling betrayed and depressed. In each case, a personal issue had become a marital crisis that involved both partners. The initial problem in one partner often starts a vicious circle. The more depressed Susan becomes, the more angry Paul becomes, demanding that she "do something." The more angry Paul becomes, the more depressed Susan becomes.

Ben and Karen got caught in such a vicious circle. Ben began to drink more and more with co-workers, trying to make friends and be accepted as "one of the guys." Karen began to nag him about drinking so much. "Look what you are doing to yourself." "You're going to lose your job and then where will we be?" "Don't you care what you are doing to us?" She then tried to control his drinking by finding where he kept his alcohol and pouring it out and by begging his friends to keep him out of bars. Finally, she decided to shame him into stopping; she began to drink with him. Ben had a drinking problem; Karen matched his problem with her attempts to make him change, to control him, to force him to become the man she wanted and needed him to be.

It is often easy to see our partner's fault in such a cycle. Karen sees the problem as being caused entirely by Ben: "I nag him and try to make him stop because he is killing himself and wrecking our marriage." Ben, on the other hand, sees Karen as the cause of the problem: "I drink because she is constantly nagging me and making my life miserable." It is not so easy for either to see what they themselves contribute to the problem. The initial problem is lost in the pattern that has developed between them. They are stuck trying to decide whose fault it is. Someone has said that to err is human and to blame it on someone else is more human. But trying to agree about who is to blame simply begins an endless and fruitless struggle to make the other admit that he or she is the one at fault. In truth, both partners usually carry some responsibility for the problem. The issue should not be who is to blame but what we can do about it. Partners need to look for solutions and not to do investigative work to decide whose fault it is. They need to offer one another large doses of understanding, support, and respect.

When a couple recognizes that both are at fault, it means that both must face the need for some kind of change. As easy as that may sound, change is hard to make. This is especially true when we do not feel very trusting or loving toward our partner. Sometimes we might try to bargain for change: "If you'll do this, then I'll change that," thinking to ourselves, *Why should I change if you are not willing to do anything to make things better?*

Covenants, however, are not based on making bargains with one another. In a covenant, we take responsibility for what we each can do. Then we step out in faith and love for one another and do what we can to change our part of the troubles we are experiencing. For Karen, that may mean refusing any longer to try to take responsibility for trying to shape Ben's life. She will love him, but she will not try to control him. She will leave his decision to drink up to him. She will no longer nag, but she will let him know how she feels and act on those feelings. If he embarrasses her in public, she will go home alone and let him find his own way home. If he wakes up sick with a hangover, he will have to call the boss himself. She will no longer do it for him and then yell at him later about it. If he frightens her and their children, she will move with them to a place where they can feel safe.

It is also helpful to develop other relationships and resources which give us renewed strength and creativity for facing our problems together. Spending time with friends and family helps restore our battered feelings about ourselves and return to our marital troubles with new perspective and energy. Finding resources that help us with the problem we are experiencing may give us new ideas and options. Karen, for example, may find important help from an Al Anon group for families of alcoholics. Susan may find it helpful to talk about her grief and depression with other family members who share some of her feelings, or with friends who have lost loved ones.

Decide Whether We Can Live
with Not Being the Perfect Couple

When imperfect people marry, they will not produce a perfect marriage. That does not mean that we should overlook the problems caused by our imperfections, but that we choose not to abandon the marriage because of them. Marriage partners hold on to one another, even when they are broken by failure and are angry because they do not meet one another's expectations. We hold on because we know that God has made us one flesh.

In *The Family Covenant*, Dennis Guernsey talks about the stages in marriage. The first stage, he says, is *romance*, when we each think that the other is perfect. If we see any faults, they are dismissed as minor. Very soon after the honeymoon, though, comes the *bargaining* stage. Partners begin to see the faults in each other more clearly and say "I'll change if you will." When this fails, partners begin *contracting*. In this stage, each tries to change the other without seeing any need to change themselves. This does not work, and they both feel disappointed and discouraged. Then they try *coercion,* trying to force one another to change. This is done with messages such as, "This marriage stinks, you have done nothing about it, and it's all your fault. If you want me to stay with you, you've got to change." Finally, spouses reach the *desperation* stage. "Nothing is going to change. I want out. But if I decide to stay with you, I'm going to give as little of myself to you as possible to keep from being hurt even more."

If couples can weather the desperation stage and recognize that neither bargaining nor contracts nor coercion can turn the other into the perfect spouse, they reach the stage of *acceptance.* Spouses accept one another, warts and all, not demanding change but promising loyalty. They no longer threaten but show commitment to one another. They love each other as real persons, and not as some romantic creation of their own imagination. At this stage, they can face their troubles together rather than blaming one another for starting the trouble in the first place.

3

How Can We Get Out of Our Marital Ruts?

As we make decisions, work through conflict that develops between us, and share our concerns and thoughts with one another, we develop patterns of dealing with things. Perhaps one partner is always the one to get angry and the other is the one who tries to soothe or who retreats into silence until the storm blows over. Or, when a major problem arises, one partner becomes helpless, and the other takes charge and sets things straight. Or, one partner may be more given to outbursts of feeling, while the other is thoughtful and more interested in facts than feelings. Our patterns help us get done what needs getting done in marriage. That is why they develop the way they do. They are like well-worn paths that lead us through conflict, stress, and decision making. They keep us from having to chart a new way of talking together every time we need to work something through.

Like all of us, Paula and Chet have such patterns. When they argue with one another, Chet is very quiet and thoughtful. He does not say much about his feelings. Paula sometimes wonders if he even has any. He seems to work almost like a computer. He takes in facts, digests them, and comes out with what he thinks is the best answer. Paula, on the other hand, pays more attention to her feelings and to the feelings of others. She makes decisions often based on how the options feel to her. Although their different styles of making decisions create some conflict for Paula and Chet, their pattern for making decisions works well most of the time. For example, when they buy a new car, Chet takes the lead, paying attention to consumer surveys, maintenance costs, and safety features. Paula trusts his judgment, although she wants some say about color and style. When it comes to something like planning a vacation with his parents, however, Paula takes more of the lead. She is sensitive to people's feelings. She thinks about such issues as family time together as well as the privacy they all will need. She takes into account what kinds of activities will be restful and enjoyable (lazing at the beach or in a mountain cabin), and what might create stress and strain relations (driving 500 miles per day across country in the same car). Chet trusts her ability to think about these options, and together they balance her knowledge about persons and feelings with his concern about the facts and figures.

Paula and Chet's patterns work for them, at least most of the time. When troubles come, or when their lives change in some way, these tried and true patterns may need to change to fit new demands on their marriage. It is during times of change or stress that we often realize that our patterns may have become ruts in which we are stuck.

The health and strength of a marriage can be gauged by looking at both the sturdiness of the patterns that have developed between partners as well as their ability to change those patterns when they need to. We often think of healthy marriages, however, as those which demonstrate certain relationship patterns, and the ways a couple may alter those patterns have, unfortunately, received less attention. For example, "The Bill Cosby Show" pictures what many people today think of as a "good" marriage. The husband and wife seem to be best friends who are able to tell each other openly what they think. When they argue, it is always in a spirit of respect, equality, and with a twinkling eye that expresses goodwill. Partners share the responsibilities of life—both cook, parent, work, do laundry. They find each other attractive. It is hinted that sex is an important and mutually enjoyable part of their relationship.

The patterns in this marriage that appeal so much to us, however, are quite different from the patterns in television marriages twenty-five years ago that were equally appealing, such as "Father Knows Best," "Leave It to Beaver," or the "Dick Van Dyke Show." In those marriages, husbands were kind and wise, humoring and protective of their more emotional and sometimes helpless wives. Conflict was rare, but when it occurred, it demonstrated these characteristics of husbands and wives. Husbands had jobs; wives were homemakers. Sex was never mentioned, and spouses slept in twin beds.

As different as these pictures are, each mirrors the values of their times. They show what is considered to be a healthy, satisfying marriage. Yet marriages take place over years, amidst changing situations and various crises. The key to a healthy marriage is whether it can weather change. In fact, long-lasting marriages almost always have to survive dramatic changes. Marriages today which may have begun as "Father Knows Best" now may look more like "The Bill Cosby Show." They have survived, changing and growing through years of amazing shifts in their patterns of living.

Healthy marriages are those that can handle change in a balanced way. Partners still hold on to old, tried and true patterns of relating that have worked well for them in the past. But they also make changes which keep them in tune with the new demands on their marriage from the world around them and from their own interpersonal world.

Marriage patterns can be pictured as paths. Healthy marriages have good paths that are straight and easy to follow. Partners can travel from conflict over a problem to its resolution using these familiar paths. Sometimes, however, these paths become ruts and partners wind up spinning their wheels. If Paula focuses *only* on feelings and Chet *only* on facts, each partner becomes one-sided. If Chet always depends on Paula to be sensitive to his feelings and the feelings of others, he will become even less sensitive to others and grow out of touch with his own values and needs. On the other side, if Paula always depends on Chet to be thoughtful and logical, she will become less able to make decisions that are based on thoughtful analysis as well as her own and others' feelings. Chet and Paula's pattern will become more and more rigid and harder to change. What would happen, for example, if Chet became seriously ill and Paula had to take over the financial decisions for the family? Or what would happen if Paula were out of town for two weeks caring for ill parents and Chet had to help their teenage daughter adjust to breaking up with her sweetheart?

It needs to be said, too, that not having any established patterns for living can create equally serious problems in a marriage. Some couples are so afraid of getting stuck in a rut that they appear to develop no patterns at all in their relationship. With every issue that comes up, they have to decide how they will decide. Conflict becomes more frequent because they do not have set patterns of relating to one another. If the baby cries in the night, they may argue about who has to get up, because they have not worked out who will do what and when. On our seminary campus, we have beautiful lawns across which students walk to class. There are signs posted which say, "Walk on the grass, but do not make paths." The grounds keepers know that people will walk on the grass, but they do not want people walking the same way again and again which will wear paths in the lawn. Some marriages are like that. Partners want to protect the lushness of their freedom, their ability to be flexible and spontaneous. As a result, they avoid making patterns with one another or even making commitments to one another.

A strong marriage, one that is healthy and can withstand change from within and from without the marriage, is a balance between freedom and responsibility, between sticking with what works and making changes. Sticking with what works gives structure to our relationship; it reminds us that we are committed to one another. But sometimes this can lead to getting stuck in a rut.

The Ruts Marriages Get Stuck In

Mistaking a Contract for Our Covenant

People often think about marriage more as a contract than as a covenant. Legally, marriage is a contract between two persons that can be ended if they do not live up to its conditions. Contracts are "if . . . then" relationships: "If you are faithful to me, I will be faithful to you and stay with you"; "If you share all your worldly goods with me, then I will share with you"; and so on. The partners in a contract state what they expect from one another at the start and must abide by their agreement if they want the contract to continue.

Covenant partners can make contracts with one another, however. God made a contract with Israel: "If you will diligently hearken to the voice of the Lord your God, and do that which is right is his eyes, and give heed to his commandments and keep all his statues, I will put none of the diseases upon you which I put upon the Egyptians; for I am the Lord, your healer" (Ex. 15:26). As important as this contract was for the well-being of the Israelites, however, it was not itself the covenant. The covenant did not end when Israel did not keep her end of the contract.

Marriage partners make agreements with one another that they expect to be honored. "If you will work for two years while I finish college, then I will work and you can go." "If you will take charge of figuring out our taxes this year, I will keep the checkbook balanced and the bills paid." Contracts can help us keep order in our lives or try new patterns of living.

If we are not careful, however, the entire marriage relationship can turn into a contract. We expect certain behaviors from our partner, for which we will return certain behaviors. We may not draw up a contract of what we expect from one another, but, though unspoken, the contract is still very real. Most American marriages include a contract for faithfulness. We expect each other not to have sexual relations with someone else. We also expect our partners to be sexually interested in us. We expect our partners to share their economic resources with us. Each marriage has its own unspoken contracts. If you want to know what your marriage contract includes, name those things your spouse might do that would make you feel betrayed or cheated. These things define you marriage contract.

When partners feel betrayed and cheated, some stop doing their part and may also pull back on their commitment. "If you are only halfheartedly meeting my needs, then I'm only going to give halfheartedly to you, too." "If you are unfaithful to me, then I'll be unfaithful to you."

Partners may, on the other hand, try to force the partner to live up to their part of the contract with threats of some kind. If threats fail, they may search for other ways to get their needs met outside of the marriage. Perhaps an investment in someone else or some new interest will bring greater reward. Contracts are based on two parties exchanging what they need from each other. If partners think they can find a better deal elsewhere, contracts are ended.

Measuring the Marriage by Other People's Standards

"Why can't you be like so-and-so's wife/husband?" is an unspoken question in the minds of some spouses that may even be voiced in the heat of a marital squabble. This question reveals that spouses are trying to cut their own relationship out of a pattern developed to fit some other couple. They read books about ideal marriages and then try to make their marriage fit that ideal. They read or hear that husbands are supposed to do certain things, and wives are supposed to do certain things. They then treat their partner as if they were some kind of wax figure playing the role of "husband" or "wife," and not as a unique person with special needs and gifts. This can lead to problems when the partner does not fit the mold we imagine that he or she should fit. It can lead to even greater problems when we try to force them into that mold.

Confusing Stability with Refusing to Change

Walt Disney has produced a cassette tape from the movie *The Fox and the Hound,* that our children used to listen to over and over on long trips in the car. The story is about a hound dog puppy and an orphaned fox kit who become best of friends and pledge to be friends forever. Naturally, life pulls them apart; and the grown hound dog is forced by his master to hunt the fox. They end up protecting each other at the risk of their lives. The fox saves the hound from a bear, and the hound stands in front of his master's gun aimed at the fox. The end of the story recalls their young voices pledging friendship forever. They kept their childhood pledge to one another, even though the outcome was far different from what they imagined their friendship would mean in the beginning. In the beginning, they simply wanted to stay playmates forever. In the end, they were not playing games but dealing with life and death.

In some ways, marriage is like this children's story. In the thrill of romance, we pledge our lives to one another, to be loyal and loving for richer or for poorer, in sickness and in health. We do not always grasp the immensity of the commitment we are making. And, like Peter Pan, we would like to freeze time and refuse to grow up. When our spouse changes, and the playfulness of the honeymoon gives way to some of the serious struggles of life, we may feel somehow betrayed. We do not want things to change. We want things to be like they used to be when our hearts were all aflutter with love.

The refusal to accept change in marriage is really an attack on the covenant of marriage. It mistakenly believes that marriage is based on unreliable feelings and trappings of love instead of the unseen structure of loyalty and sharing of all of life, even through troubled waters. Couples need the security and stability that comes from knowing that they can depend on one another no matter how they might feel, no matter what circumstances might be thrust upon them, or no matter what changes they might choose to make in their life together.

Making Changes in Marriage

In order to survive, living things must grow. With growth comes change. Each day, our bodies grow new cells and get rid of dead ones. The faces of fifty-year-old people only bear a faint resemblance to the little kids of forty-four years before. The marriage relationship, too, is a living thing. The two have become one flesh, but the way of all flesh is to change. Marriages must grow and change in order to survive. Therefore, a fifteen-year-old marriage probably only faintly resembles the honeymoon couple of fifteen years before.

Healthy marriages can change when necessary. They are flexible and bend in different shapes to fit their circumstances

(Lewis and others, 1979; Lewis & Looney, 1983). They show this flexibility by:

Being Sensitive to the Unique Needs and Strengths of Partners

Effective change in marriage requires that we know one another and ourselves well, and that we trust one another enough to be unlike any so-called ideal marriage or any other couple we might know. It may result in looking odd to others. In chapter 2, we talked about Adam, the husband who wants to leave his business to go into forestry. Perhaps Adam and Jane may decide that he will take a leave of absence from work and spend three months working on a forestry project to try out his dream, and Jane will join him on weekends when she can. They do not know where their dream will lead them, and friends may think that they are crazy. But they will struggle to remain committed to each other even in unusual circumstances.

Being Tuned in to the Demands of the World Around Them

Two friends were trying to find their way around St. Louis. One friend was driving and the other was looking at the map and giving directions. They could not find their way and seemed to be going in circles. In exasperation, the driver looked over and exclaimed, "That's not a map of St. Louis! That's a map of Louisville!" Sometimes we try to find our way through the unfamiliar territory of changing circumstances in marriage using the wrong map, a map of another time and place in our life together. We need to check whether that old map is of any use by looking around us and finding landmarks that will help us get our bearings.

If we have a map of other people's experiences, it may help us find our own way. A couple struggling with the problem of a teenager abusing drugs, for example, may find the experiences of other parents helpful. But it is most important to be sensitive to the needs and problems in the life of their own child and their own family. Someone else's map may not work. Couples need to know their own territory and they must make their own path through it.

Understanding and Accepting Stress
When Partners Are Coping with Change

Change creates stress for all of us. In a healthy marriage, partners give one another extra room when they are struggling with a problem or a crisis in the marriage or the family. They know that moodiness, forgetfulness, and short tempers are part of going through change.

Facing Change Together

In healthy marriages, partners find ways to support one another, even when they do not have a direct role in the change effort. They communicate in no uncertain terms, "we're in this together."

Looking to the Future

Couples should look to the future and what they can do together rather than blaming one another for the difficulties that change presents. When partners are trying to make needed changes, it is tempting to get sidetracked into arguing about who's to blame for problems, who got us into this, and who is having to make the greatest sacrifice to get us out of it. In a healthy marriage, each partner takes responsibility for him or herself, as we discussed in chapter 2, and refrains from trying to blame the partner. Instead, the focus is on "Where do we go from here?"

Communicating Their Love and Commitment to One Another Clearly and Often

When hot words have been exchanged and each feels weighted down by the challenge they face together, partners in healthy marriages find ways to remind one another of their commitment and faith in their covenant: "I love you; I know we'll make it through this." They show it in actions that lift each other up and keep the problem from taking over their marriage.

Risking New Patterns in Their Relationship

Change requires risk. Partners in healthy marriages feel secure enough with one another that they can risk doing things that might make them feel uncomfortable. They trust one another not to laugh or criticize their attempts to do things differently. Paula, the feeling, intuitive wife, and Chet, the thinking, logical husband we mentioned at the beginning of this chapter, will need to make some changes if their well-worn pattern does not become a rut. Chet will need to learn the value of his own feelings as important information for making decisions. He also needs to learn to tune into the feelings of others. Paula needs to develop her own abilities to make logical, thoughtful decisions. Each will need to encourage the other, supporting their first efforts at making decisions differently even if those first efforts are clumsy.

Dealing with Feelings in Ways That Build the Relationship

Partners in healthy marriages recognize the power of feelings for either building or destroying a relationship. Because partners share so much of their lives, the opportunity for conflict and anger to arise is always present. Partners need to control and express their anger in ways that help them work

through conflict and build up their marriage rather than destroy it. They also need to refrain from using drugs or alcohol
or other escapes to avoid dealing with the strong feelings that
marital conflict often creates. We will look with more detail at
the role of conflict and anger in marriage in chapter 4.

Problems in Making Changes

Protecting our commitment to one another is difficult, and
we have described some of the problems that face couples who
try to keep their marriage strong and stable. Making changes,
however, can also create problems for couples. Some ruts are so
deep that we may shake a marriage apart trying to escape
them. We will look at some of the problems couples face in
trying to make changes.

We Don't See Our Need for Change

Change is frightening. It means leaving behind what used to
work and striking out in a new direction. The ruts may indeed
be ruts, but at least they are our ruts. Sometimes change
frightens us so much that we refuse even to admit our need to
make a change. Sarah and Tom were like that. Tom felt his
manhood was at stake in being able to support Sarah in the
way he thought a husband should. To admit that he needed
help, that he perhaps could not protect her and support her as
he wanted, was more than he could face. In the same way,
Sarah had equated in her mind being cared for with being
loved. She wanted so much to feel loved that she could not face
the fact that there was also a part of her that needed to have a
share in controlling their life together. It was only when their
world came crashing around them with the threat of losing
their home that they had to make a change in the way they did
things.

Sometimes couples make a silent agreement to overlook their

need to change. They close their eyes to the problems in their relationship. Both may be so afraid of conflict that they avoid it at all cost. They may allow their relationship to wither and die because they cannot bring themselves to begin working on their differences. If such a couple has children, their child may begin acting out at home, getting into trouble at school, creating problems in the neighborhood, or using drugs. The child carries the heavy burden of the family's silent conflict. By acting out, it is almost as if the child is expressing the conflict for the parents. By giving the parents a focus for their troubles, the child forces them to pull together if only to try to deal with the child's problem. Children may try to make things right with Mommy and Daddy, but they cannot save their parents' marriages. Only when parents begin to face the troubles in the marriage themselves can creative change take place.

We Don't Let Each Other Know Our Need for Change

A partner may be very aware of the problems in the marriage but not be able to share this need so that the spouse understands the problem.

Jesus taught us to ask, seek, and knock (Luke 11:9), even though God knows what we need before we ever ask (Matt. 6:8). Our partners are not nearly as omniscient as God. They cannot read our minds—although sometimes we think they should. We need to tell them what is on our mind.

Partners not only need to ask for what they need; they need also to ask in ways that their spouses can hear them. Paul encouraged us in Ephesians 4:15 to *speak the truth in love*. This is particularly important for marriage partners. We are to face the truth of the troubles in our relationship in ways that respect both partners' needs. One should avoid exaggerating the truth to make self look good or make the partner look guilty. We need to avoid words like "always" and "never." ("You always

tell the children that *I* say they can't do something, even
though we agree." "You never call me to tell me you're going to
be late; you never think about how worried I might be.")
Rarely are statements with "always" and "never" true. They
simply make my partner more defensive and make it harder
for us to understand one another.

Paul continued in Ephesians 4:29 to advise, "Let no evil talk
come out of your mouths, but only such as is good for edifying,
as fits the occasion, that it may impart grace to those who
hear." This also applies to the marriage relationship. We need
to share our needs for change in the relationship in ways that
build up our love and commitment to one another, not in ways
that undermine it. We want to win the victory over the trouble
we are experiencing, not over our partner.

A partner can hear us better if we choose a time and place
"as fits the occasion" (Eph. 4:29). Therefore, we need to be
wise when choosing times to share our needs. Snatches of time
at the end of the day when both are tired are not the best times
to struggle with difficult issues. This should be done when
both partners are at their strongest and can give their best to
the task of working together on troubles.

In telling my partner about how I see the need for change in
our marriage, I must recognize that my partner may see things
quite differently. The respect for differences that is such an
important part of our covenant requires that I let my partner
know that this is what *I* think or feel, and that I know that
there are probably other ways to see things. For example, I
might say, "When you and I disagree, we usually end up doing
things my way. I like being in control, and I think I make good
decisions. But I don't like it when you later blame me if things
go wrong." This is quite different from assuming that I see the
whole picture, that my viewpoint is the whole truth: "When
we disagree, you always give in. You let me run the show because you're afraid of taking responsibility, and then you can

blame me when things go wrong." The first way communicates respect. The second way communicates scorn, "I know more about you than you know yourself."

Finally, if we want to be successful in letting one another know our need for change, we must be able to listen as well as talk. Listening means more that being quiet and recording in my brain the words of my partner. It means that I must use those words as clues in creating in my imagination what my partner things and feels, what it is like to be my partner. If I truly listen, I have to stop thinking about what I am going to say as soon as my partner stops to take a breath and to start thinking about what my partner is trying to tell me. In marital quarrels, we must remember, "A fool takes no pleasure in understanding, but only in expressing his opinion" (Prov. 18:2).

We Know We Need to Change But Can't Agree on How

Surprisingly, once we begin to understand each other, some problems seem to evaporate. Even if problems remain, the feeling of being understood and cared for that comes from the fact that my partner has listened to me respectfully and lovingly gives renewed strength for coping.

More serious troubles in marriage, however, do not go away simply by understanding our own needs and the needs of one another. Ben and Karen still face the problem of Ben's alcohol abuse. Karen must still struggle to support and love him even though she recognizes that trying to force him to change or to protect him from his alcohol dependency does not help. Understanding is part of the battle, but it does not end the war. It is the first step, but how can we then progress in the work ahead of us?

Ways We Can Change Together

The first step in making changes is to decide together what we want to have happen in our relationship. What do we each need from the other? Ben and Karen may decide that Ben needs to take responsibility for his drinking. She is frightened that he is ruining his life but feels powerless to do anything about it. Ben does not believe that it is as big a problem as Karen makes it out to be, and he wants her to let him decide for himself if and when he will drink.

Once they have defined the first step of what they want to have happen, a couple can begin to think of possible ways they can work on taking the first step. Both need to recognize that this is not the final answer. Karen wants Ben to stop drinking, and she is unsure if she will be satisfied with anything less. But she has to respect him by allowing him to control his own life. In the same way, Ben has to respect her need for control in her life and to recognize how powerless his drinking makes her feel. For example, he must realize that, among other things, she does not want to be embarrassed by him in public. He must realize that she is worried about what this is doing to their children.

As partners work toward possible steps they can take, it helps if each concentrates on what *I* can do and less on what *you* can do. Ben volunteers that he will no longer drink when they are out together or around the children. Karen says that she will no longer pour out the liquor she finds. He says that he is willing to go to a weekly Alcoholics Anonymous meeting, and she agrees to go with him to attend the Al-Anon meeting for family members across the hall.

Partners need to remember that they are not necessarily going to arrive at the best solution immediately. Often, the "best" solution depends on who is naming it. Karen's best solution would be for Ben to stop drinking, period. Ben's best solution would be for Karen to leave him alone about it. Neither of these solutions, however, will be agreed upon by both. For either to insist or to try to force their own solutions would not communicate respect and loyalty.

Contracts can be useful tools in beginning to change together, so long as a couple remembers that the contract is a way of experimenting with ways of changing and is not a test of the marriage. Some basic guidelines in using contracts include:

Make the Contract Positive

Contracts need to look ahead to what will be different in our marriage and not look back on the old behavior that we want to change. Ben may contract, for example, to "drink only soft drinks when we are out in public together," a positive change. A negative contract focuses on what is wrong, such as "I'll stop embarrassing you in public," and not on what we want to make right. Negative contracts are not as helpful since they focus on what can go wrong, not on our hope and commitment to one another for a changed future.

State What You Want Your Partner to Do, Not What You Want Your Partner to Make You Feel

Partners often ask their partners to make them feel a certain way, such as "I wish you were more romantic" or "I wish you would stop embarassing me" or "I wish you respected my feelings more." Each of these wishes can mean a lot of different things. They do not tell the partner specifically what to do or not to do. It helps to tell our partners exactly what we want them to do or say. For example, the message "I wish you were more romantic" might be clearer if the request were made in this way, "I wish you would wear something pretty when you are with me in the evenings instead of that old pink bathrobe." Or, "I wish we could turn off the TV this evening and take a walk or sit on the porch together like we used to do." Or, "I wish you would surprise me sometime with a flower or a little gift or a love note hidden someplace where I will find it." Our spouses are more likely to do what we need or want from them if we spell out our request clearly.

In the same way, we can be much clearer in our contracts with our partner for change if we state specifically what we are going to do. If Karen were to say, "I will treat you with more respect," that could mean something very different to Ben than it does to Karen, leading to feelings of disappointment or anger later. Instead, she might say, "I will leave your liquor alone. I will not talk about your drinking unless you bring it up first. I will expect you to take care of the consequences of your drinking yourself: I will not call your boss when you don't feel like going to work, and I will not bring you aspirin when you have a hangover."

Make Sure Both Partners Are Giving Something to the Other

It is clear that this trouble belongs mostly to Ben and that it is a serious problem. But Ben and Karen are partners. Karen needs to try to find ways that she can change that will support the changes Ben is trying to make. She is not threating to do something if he does not change; she is giving of herself to help him with his problem.

Set Time Limits

If all they were going to do about the problem is for Ben to stop drinking in public and Karen to stop nagging him about it, Karen would probably not agree to this contract. A contract should be a chance to try to handle a problem in a new way for a period of time which is agreed upon by both. The problem may look different a few days or weeks into their contract. At the end of the time period, which they set for four weeks, Ben and Karen need a chance to think and talk together about what they have done and felt. They may continue with the same actions they have started, or they may need to go in a different direction. Contracts are not forever.

Keep the Contract in Its Proper Place

It is too easy to let the contract take the place of the covenant. If Ben gets drunk at the next party that they attend, Karen may be tempted to go home, pack a suitcase, and leave. But a contract is only an attempt to create change in a relationship. It is not the relationship itself. When contracts fail, we need to deal with our anger and disappointment; but this should not mark the end of our loyalty and love for one another. At some point, Karen may indeed decide that separation or divorce is the best answer for her, their children, and for Ben if their relationship deteriorates into mutual destruction from which they cannot seem to escape. She will not decide this, however, in order to punish Ben for failing to meet his end of some contract they have worked out.

Contracts are merely steps in a long journey toward change in troubled marriages. They may or may not help. If they are successful, they offer hope that we can change things, however slowly. Like contracts, this chapter—this book—offers first steps. Couples troubled by marital problems will not find change easy. The ideas in this chapter do not provide all that they will need in their working toward a solution together. But when we accept the commitment of our marriage covenant, with God's help, all things are possible.

4

How Can We Keep Anger from Wrecking Our Marriage?

There are few people who can make us angrier than our marriage partners. In many marriages, the most common feeling between spouses is anger, not love. Angry feelings can flare up over the smallest issues. A coffee cup left in the wrong place, a certain look, or showing up ten minutes late may set off a raging conflict that leads to threats of separation. How is it that seemingly insignificant problems can blow sky high?

First, even though such issues may seem small, they are right next to our skin, rubbing and chafing each time we move. Did you ever put on a new shirt and wear it somewhere, only to realize too late that a little plastic tag was still attached inside the collar? All day long, it rubs the inside of your neck and irritates you. You may try tucking it under somehow, or pulling it out, but nothing seems to work short of taking off the shirt and cutting the tag out with scissors. It is so small, but it is constantly with you.

Marriage problems are similar. We share our bed, our bathroom, our kitchen, our closet—all the places where we live day in and day out—with our partner. If a problem comes up, we cannot seem to get away from it. It constantly rubs and irritates. David Mace has said that differences between people become disagreements when space is limited (Mace, 1982). If I believe that everything should be in its proper place, I may smile at a friend's messy house. If my partner, however, leaves a mess all over my living space, that is another issue altogether. So much of what each of us does as an individual affects the other. If I forget to put gas in the car, my partner may run out on the freeway the next morning. If I splurge on new clothes, there may not be enough money for my partner's college tuition.

Second, because marriage partners are expected to share a bed, a house, a checkbook, and practically everything else except a toothbrush, they have to do a lot of coordinating. Much serious marital conflict comes from problems in working out the daily patterns of living together. These gripes may sound familiar: "It drives me crazy when you don't record the amount of the checks you write." "I just cleaned up the kitchen; now look at it!" "If you want to stay up late and read, the least you can do is to go into the family room and let me turn out the light and go to sleep!" In many ways, our daily life together is like a dance. We have to work out some patterns that we both know and agree to or we will be stepping all over one another's toes.

One of the biggest areas of coordination required in marriage is managing the family household. In a national survey, Murray Straus found that the issue that causes the most conflict in marriage is housework. For example, one third of American couples said that they *always* disagree about cooking and cleaning. And this does not count all the couples who only *sometimes* disagree about these daily tasks (Straus, Gelles, & Steinmetz, 1980).

Such coordination does not sound so difficult. After all, how hard can it be to make plans such as "If you cook, I'll clean up the kitchen later," or "I'll try to keep my mess out of the living room and dining room, if I can have one place where I can leave my stuff spread out like I want it." If it were just a matter of developing a reasonable plan, it would not be so hard.

When spouses are planning their daily patterns, however, more is happening than meets the eye. For one thing, the partners are not just discussing clean kitchens and where to put piles of papers or unfinished projects; they are talking about how much power each has over the other. Sometimes the power issues are hard to see, but they are present. For example, the partner who says, "If you cook, I'll clean up the kitchen later" may also be giving the message, "I get to sit down and read the paper while you cook, and I'll clean up the kitchen when I feel like it. I will not give you the power to make me feel bad for not helping you with dinner." The spouse with the pile of papers may be saying, "You are in control of most of our life together, but there are still corners of my life that are mine over which you have no power."

We often feel anger rise when our partner's actions make us feel robbed in some way of control in our own life. And few people in our lives have more power over us. By spending too long in the shower, one partner can keep the other from having hot water for a bath. By leaving the scissors in a strange place, one partner can keep the other hunting in exasperation for thirty minutes. By spending too much money on some spur-of-the-moment purchase, one can keep the other from buying the new winter coat for which they had been saving.

Power is therefore often a hidden agenda in these "small" issues that cause such big conflicts. Another issue is whether or not we feel loved. Working out patterns for living together in marriage is not like negotiating a business deal. In business relationships, each person drives a hard bargain and tries to get all they can out of the other. Both parties are expected to look out for themselves. When the hard bargaining is over, they let one another know with a smile, a pat on the back, or a handshake that it was nothing personal, just good business.

In marriage, however, partners are not expected to try to get the best deal for themselves. They are expected to suggest a plan that looks out for the best interests of the other and not just themselves. As covenant partners, each is to give of the self for the other without counting the cost. A partner does not enter a covenant to drain the other dry.

When we think our partners are acting selfishly or ignoring our needs, we become enraged because we feel used and unloved. It is not just kitchen duty that is at stake, but our very covenant may be questioned. Of all the people in the world, my covenant partner is supposed to act in ways that support me and show consideration of my needs. When my partner leaves me a car to drive with an empty gas tank, I not only feel a loss of power over my life—I had planned just enough time to get to work and now I will be late—I may also feel unloved. "If she loved me, she would have been thoughtful enough to put gas in the car after her trip."

As marriages become more troubled, spouses interpret more and more of one another's behavior as a comment on the marriage. They do not allow each other to make mistakes or to be forgetful without thinking that it says something about the marriage: "If you really love me (care about me, respect me), you would not leave your clothes in the bathroom floor for me to pick up." Partners then get confused about what the issue is: do we need to talk about picking up clothes in the bathroom, or whether we love one another?

Conflict in marriage comes from other sources as well. Some of it derives from differences in the partners' basic values. One partner may believe in living each day to the fullest; the other may want to plan for tomorrow and save for a rainy day. Unless one simply gives in, they will have to come face-to-face with their conflict. Value differences are hard to work through, because our values are important to us or they would not be values. They also can carry messages about who has the power in the marriage, or who is the most loving and understanding because he or she is willing to compromise or give in.

Value differences may be all wrapped up in how we coordinate our daily lives. Consequently, we cannot seem to tackle one issue without pulling in all the rest. A simple disagreement about whether we should try to paint the house ourselves or hire professional painters may involve (1) our values about money and time, and how they should be spent; (2) who makes decisions, and how we each think decisions ought to be made; (3) who "wins," and what that means about who has the power in our marriage; and (4) the degree to which we each feel that our partner understands our feelings, and loves us by hearing us out and taking our thoughts about the issue seriously.

Another issue which creates trouble in many marriages is the difference in how much partners want to share of themselves with one another. One partner may want to share every thought, every feeling, every waking moment. The other may want to protect some privacy and search for ways to be alone in the midst of their shared life. Unfortunately, it is sometimes hard for partners to see that they are simply different from each other. Instead, they may think their conflict is about whether they love one another. The sharing partner feels unloved and shut out. The private partner feels smothered. As the sharing partner tries to move closer, the private partner moves away. Both may become increasingly frustrated and angry.

Conflict itself does not create trouble in marriage. It is a necessary ingredient in marriage. Research indicates that partners who experience greater satisfaction in their marriage also have a lot of conflict (Argyle & Furnham, 1983). On the other hand, troubled marriages also often contain a lot of conflict. In understanding the role of conflict in troubled marriages, we must first realize that it is not whether couples have conflict that makes for happy or troubled marriages. Instead, it is how they handle that conflict. Partners may find conflict to be a source of creative change in their relationship that brings them closer together, or they may find that it leads to destruction of their love and commitment to one another. One of the deciding factors in whether conflict will be constructive or destructive is the way the partners handle the anger which often is the lightning and thunder that go with the storms of conflict.

What's Wrong with Anger?

"Anger" is the meaning persons give to changes they experience in their bodies when they sense danger. We sense danger when we think we may lose something important to us, or when we feel out of control of our own lives. A marriage partner has countless ways of making the other feel this loss of control. I may settle down with a glass of iced tea and the Sunday paper in the late afternoon, only to find that my partner has read the paper first and cut out several sections that include what I want to read. I have lost something that I had been counting on. Or we may be enjoying a dinner with friends when my partner begins to tell a story about something stupid I did. Everyone laughs, but I feel my confidence has been betrayed as a private joke has just been made public. I cannot control what other people are thinking about me. After hearing that story, they must think I am a complete idiot. Or, at the same party, I notice and am shocked to see my partner talking quietly and closely with a person of the opposite sex. I have never questioned the loyalty and love of my partner before, but suddenly I am afraid that there is attraction to someone else. In each case, I feel some loss of control, some threat to me and what is important to me. And my partner seems to be the one responsible for these feelings.

Anger involves three connected elements. First, something happens—I see my partner talking to someone. Second, I give an interpretation to what is happening that threatens me in some way—my partner is romantically interested in this person. Finally, my body goes through changes to prepare to respond to the threat. My heart pounds, my muscles tighten, the blood flowing to my digestive system is restricted and goes instead to my lungs and limbs as I prepare to run away or fight off whatever is threatening me—I feel my face flush, my teeth and fists clench, and my heart is racing as I decide what to do.

These three elements are not always connected to one another in a simple line of progression (see fig. 1). For example, I may, on second glance, realize that the person my partner is talking to is a distant cousin; and they are probably talking about Aunt Suzie's latest adventure. Even though I still see my partner talking to the opposite sex, the interpretation I give to what I see is quite different. It does not lead to anger (see fig. 2).

Figure 1. Anger

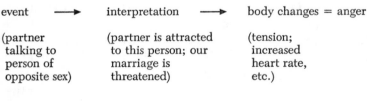

event $\longrightarrow$	interpretation $\longrightarrow$	body changes = anger
(partner talking to person of opposite sex)	(partner is attracted to this person; our marriage is threatened)	(tension; increased heart rate, etc.)

Figure 2. Anger Short-Circuited

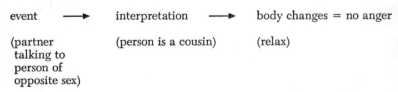

event $\longrightarrow$	interpretation $\longrightarrow$	body changes = no anger
(partner talking to person of opposite sex)	(person is a cousin)	(relax)

Another possibility is that my body may already be in a state of tension which has nothing to do with my marriage. I did not sleep well the night before; the boss told me today that if I did not increase my sales I could look for another job; and I got a speeding ticket on the way home. A very small event may be just the right target at which I can vent all the tension which has been building up inside me. It is much easier, after all, to explode in anger at a marriage partner than it is at the boss, the police officer, or even at our children who are fussy and tired after a long day. My partner will not fire me (like my boss), or put me in jail (like the policeman), or be too small to understand that my anger does not mean that I have stopped loving them (like my children).

Marriage seems to be the safest of all places to get angry. But it also has its own danger. When my wife asks me to run to the grocery late in the evening, I may use this as an excuse that allows all my pent-up tension to come bursting out. "How can you ask this of me! I have worked hard all day, spent all evening with the kids reading stories and getting them settled in bed. When I finally get to sit down for a few minutes, you're at me again. If you would just plan better, I wouldn't have to make all these little trips out. We spend way too much as it is on groceries. I've told you and told you that you have got to learn to budget better. What's it going to take to get through to you? You'll just have to make do!" The longer I talk, the more meaning I attach to my wife's request and the hotter I get. By the time I have finished ranting, I have tied the reason for all of my tension (which has built up through the day) to the request of my spouse to run to the store.

The longer I rant, the more tense and more upset I feel until I am in a full-blown rage. The interpretation I have given to this simple request not only explains the tension I feel; it makes me even more tense. By the time I have finished blaming my wife for everything I am feeling, I am even more upset than before. The process began, then, with body tension which simply needed the spark of an event to explode. The end result is the same—anger.

Figure 3. Body Tension

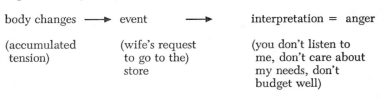

Spouses in troubled marriages often feel a lot of tension in their lives that does not derive from their marriages. It is like kindling waiting for a match. Perhaps they are still struggling with problems in the family in which they grew up. Or relationships at work or with the children may build up pressure. Or health or mental health problems may keep them feeling strained. When people live with such continuing sources of stress, much smaller events can serve as the spark that ignites anger in the marriage. The slightest glance, the poorly timed request, or even silence when one thinks the other ought to be talking, may push them into anger (Tavris, 1982).

Second, in troubled marriages, partners often live with uncertainty. Because they have troubles, they are constantly on the lookout for signs of more trouble. They expect it. Almost every event can be given a variety of interpretations; but in a troubled marriage, partners often assume that the worst possible interpretation is the "real" one.

For example, dirty clothes left in the bathroom floor can be interpreted to mean, "He was really tired and forgot to pick up after himself." Or they can mean, "He is so used to his mother picking up after him that he doesn't think about picking up after himself." Or one can conclude, "He knows that if he leaves them there, I'll pick them up; he has me trained"; or

"He assumes it is my job to wait on him; he thinks I am his servant and doesn't care how I feel." In a troubled marriage, a partner is likely to assume that the worst meaning is the "real" one. The wife who finds dirty clothes on the floor is looking for clues to confirm how troubled their marriage really is and how their love and concern for one another is drying up. The clothes on the floor may be there for several or all of the explanations listed. But if the partner attaches the last meaning to it, the marriage is just as troubled as the partner thinks it is, even though that might have little to do with the husband's own interpretation of his clothes on the bathroom floor.

Anger is, therefore, considerably more complex than a simple feeling that we have that needs to be expressed. By giving meaning to what we experience in our life together, we actually give shape to and control the way our relationship develops (Meichenbaum & Turk, 1976; Tavris, 1982). As we have described it so far, anger includes the interpretation we give to events in life. It is not simply a feeling that comes over us. Anger is also what we *choose to do*. We interpret something that has happened. Then we express our interpretation by yelling, crying, slamming a cabinet door, withdrawing in silence, or by calmly and rationally talking about it.

This definition of anger fits a biblical understanding of anger found in James 1:20. The writer cautions us to be "quick to hear, slow to speak, slow to anger, for the anger of man does not work the righteousness of God." The anger he is talking about is not a feeling inside ourselves, because we cannot control how slowly or quickly we feel. Feelings simply come. What we can control, however, is how open we are to understanding what happens to us in our relationship. We can take time to see things from viewpoints different from the most incriminating one. We can also choose how we will express to our partner what has happened and what we think and feel about it. We can yell about it, or we can talk about it.

Anger is an important warning light in marriage that something is wrong. It signals that we have a problem. The problem may be that one partner is under such stress from other areas of life that tension is leaking into the marriage, or that one partner is so upset about the marriage that every wrong move seems to shake it to its foundation, or that our expectations and needs are not being met. When the oil light flashes on the dashboard of your car, you need to take steps to fix the problem. Anger signals that partners need to take action to locate the problem in their relationship and do something about it. Too often, however, anger becomes more than the warning light that something is amiss but the very trouble that threatens the marriage.

How Anger Can Trouble a Marriage

It is not unusual for couples to talk about their marital troubles as problems they cannot solve: "We seem so distant from one another and don't seem to have anything in common"; "We have such different values"; "Her parents interfere in our marriage and she won't put a stop to it"; "We disagree about everything from soap to sex." Many times, couples believe these to be unsolvable problems because whenever they try to work their way through the trouble, anger arises and blocks their way. Anger can block the partners' ability to handle differences and can become a serious problem whenever it takes on a life of its own, when partners do not act like partners, when winning the fight is more important than upholding the marriage covenant, and when it keeps partners from finding creative ways to make needed changes.

When Anger Takes on a Life of Its Own
Many people believe that they need to express their feelings if they are to be physically and emotionally healthy. One needs

to let off steam, they think. They believe that not expressing anger leads to physical illness such as ulcers or emotional distress such as depression. The "getting it out of your system" approach, however, has an opposite effect from what we might intend—it makes the anger grow. Tavris reports that giving free rein to our feelings does not get rid of the feelings; it just makes them stronger (Tavris, 1982). Since one key element in anger is the bodily changes that prepare us to run or fight, it makes sense that yelling, throwing things, talking it out, or even the silence behind clenched teeth increase the stress our bodies feel. How many times have you heard someone say, "The more I thought about it, the madder I got."

The problem with venting anger is that anger is given a life of its own. The interpretation I have given to events and the desire to get things off my chest take center stage. Instead of focusing on our marital relationship and the problems we need to tackle together, I am focused on what I am thinking and feeling. Anger becomes the problem and not simply a warning signal that points to a problem.

When the Bible condemns anger, it is this kind of anger that is in view. "A man of quick temper acts foolishly, but a man of discretion is patient" (Prov. 14:17). "He who is slow to anger has great understanding, but he who has a hasty temper exalts folly" (v. 29). "Be not quick to anger, for anger lodges in the bosom of fools" (Eccl. 7:9). In being quick to express anger, we blurt out our own feelings without taking the time to understand what is happening from our partner's perspective. We ignore how our anger can be used in the service of our covenant.

Anger that takes on a life of its own often becomes hostile and vengeful, either physically or emotionally. Most murder and violence in this country takes place among family members. Each year, in one out of ten American marriages, one spouse beats up the other (Straus, Gelles, & Steinmetz, 1980). The Bible warns that anger that is given free rein will lead to murder. Jesus even equates anger with murder (Matt. 5:22). If we give someone a look that could kill, the next step is to kill them. Cain killed his brother Abel in anger, because the Lord accepted Abel's gift and rejected Cain's (Gen. 4:4-8). In a fit of anger, Moses killed an Egyptian and had to run for his life (Ex. 2:11-15). Saul's anger led to his murderous pursuit of David. Absalom's rage at his half-brother Amnon for raping Absalom's sister fed his plot to kill Amnon (2 Sam. 13).

Even if partners never touch each other in anger, they can rub each other out with a cutting remark and a hateful look. We can communicate our wish that the other did not exist. In our thoughts we commit murder. It is clear that James was right: "the anger of man does not work the righteousness of God" (Jas. 1:20).

Paul quoted Psalm 4:4 in Ephesians 4:26: "Be angry, but sin not." Does this mean that we can be angry as long as we do not sin? In English, the words "be angry" sound like a command; go ahead and be angry. The psalm, however, meant something quite different from this. In Hebrew, the phrase implies, "*If you are angry*, do not let anger lead you into sin" (NEB, authors' italics; see Barth, 1974). Just five verses later, Paul told us to put away all bitterness, temper, and anger, along with all malice (v. 31; see also Col. 3:8). For Paul, anger is not something we are ordered to feel or express. It is dangerous and can lead us to sin. It is something that Satan can easily use to destroy us and those around us (Eph. 4:27; see also 2 Cor. 12:20; Gal. 5:20; Col. 3:8; 1 Tim. 2:8; Titus 1:7). God warned Cain when he was angry that sin was crouching at the door, waiting for a chance to spring (Gen. 4:7). Cain did not heed the warning. As a result, he killed his brother, Abel, in a rage.

Anger can be given a life of its own by using it as an excuse to lash out at each other with hurtful words and actions. It can also take over our marriage when we hold it inside. Perhaps no word passes our lips; but inside we nurse the anger, turning it over and over in our minds. We allow it to take control of our thoughts about each other. Like cancer, the anger grows, silently destroying our relationship. We may even pride ourselves in our self-control, that we are somehow above yelling or other forms of expressing anger. Paul warned, "Do not let the sun go down on your anger" (Eph. 4:26). For the Hebrews, the day ended at sunset. Paul told us to pay attention to the anger and do something with it before the day is through. Do not allow the anger itself to ruin tomorrow and eventually the life of our covenant together.

When Spouses Do Not Act Like Partners

When anger sets off the alarm that all is not well, partners need to find the problem and figure out how to deal with it. Often, the problem involves differences in the spouses' values or beliefs or needs. In order to work through the problem, the views of each partner needs to be expressed and included in any solution. In other words, marriage requires two strong individuals who can stand face-to-face, as equals, and work through their differences.

First Samuel 24 records a story of conflict and intrigue between Saul and David. Saul pursued David into the wilderness in a search-and-destroy mission. As the story goes, he entered a cave alone in order to relieve himself, unaware that David and his men were hiding there in the dark. David's men urged him to kill Saul. Instead, David crept up behind Saul and cut off the skirt of his robe without Saul ever knowing what had happened. Saul left the cave having no idea that anyone else was about. Afterwards, David came to Saul and presented him with the skirt of his robe. By doing this, he showed Saul how easily he could have killed him. Then, David laid down his sword. In response to this, Saul wept; and they restored (temporarily, at least) their relationship.

David did not force Saul to grovel on the ground and beg for mercy. He did not handle the anger between them by trying to overpower Saul and destroy him, or by giving in. Instead, David chose to continue to be a faithful friend of King Saul in spite of Saul's anger. David showed Saul that they were equals. But David chose to show his equality in such a way that he did not make Saul seem less powerful than he.

In the face of an angry marriage partner, many choose to try to destroy the other with cutting remarks or by making the partner look like a fool. They try to force the other to give in. Sometimes, the anger of one partner leads to even greater anger in the other. Partners declare war on each other instead of on the problem that separates them.

Other partners may choose instead to give in no matter what, just to end the conflict. They may say that they are doing this out of meekness or love. But the marriage can be weakened when one partner caves in to the other's anger. The partner may want to keep peace at any cost, but the marriage loses in the end because spouses are no longer partners. Instead, they become a drill sergeant and a buck private. We may be afraid to stand up to one another like David did with Saul. But it is only when we respect each other as equals who have choices that we can then work through problems in a way that will enable us to come out stronger as a couple.

Christians often think it is their duty as Christians to give in. Usually, it is the wife who is expected or who expects herself to take a weaker role. Some quote Ephesians 5:24, "Let wives be subject in everything to their husbands," as a proof text for subservience. They interpret this to mean that wives are supposed to knuckle under to their husbands in all things. In our opinion, this is not what Paul intended. The entire chapter in Ephesians needs to be read to understand what Paul was saying. When a marital storm brews and the husband is angry, Paul did not intend for the Christian wife to roll over and play dead. Being submissive does not mean that the wife allows the husband to have his way.

First, we must recognize that wives are told to be submissive to their husbands "as to the Lord" (v. 22). This means that she is to be responsible *first* to Christ in every part of her life, including marriage. She is to live out her commitment to Christ in her relationship with her husband.

Second, "submission" is not the same thing as "obedience." The word *obey* is not used in verse 22; in fact, no verb occurs in the Greek text. It reads literally, "Wives to your husbands as to the Lord." We can assume that the verb in 5:24, "submit," is to be supplied. In chapter 6, children are told to obey their parents (v. 1) and slaves to obey their masters (v. 5), but wives are not told to obey their husbands. To be submissive means to be humble and unselfish. It means that we consider the needs of the other first. We can see that David was submissive even when he stood up to Saul. He did not try to destroy or embarrass him. He was humble before Saul. But he was also strong and courageous. He confronted Saul, but in a spirit of love that restored their relationship instead of destroying it.

It is tempting to roll over and "play dead" in marriage and call that submission. It is easier than confronting an angry partner. It is easy to allow the partner to run the show. If he is angry, let him have his way and make him happy. This will result in less open conflict. It will also take less time for storms to blow over, since no time is spent struggling to reach some kind of agreement together. But such a marriage is very lonely. When one partner gets his or her way every time they get angry, spouses are not acting like partners. They do not share the burdens of the decisions they make. The storm may blow over quickly, but the problem between the partners, like a current in still water, runs deep. Often the weaker spouse who gives in stores up anger inside and begins to nurse a grudge against the other. As one wife told me, "My husband and I never argue. I always submit to whatever he wants. Then, after he leaves for work, I swish his toothbrush in the toilet."

When Winning the Fight Is More Important than Upholding the Marital Covenant

For other spouses, being submissive is the last thing they are trying to do. Instead, when they are angry, their major goal is to trounce their partner. Some Christians misinterpret Ephesians 5:23, "For the husband is the head of the wife," to mean that he is to lord it over the wife. They ignore Paul's continued important qualifier. The husband is head "as Christ is the head of the church, his body, and is himself its Savior." Christ's sacrifice of His life for His people is to be the model for the husband's relationship to his wife. Lording it over others, Jesus said, was the way of heathens (Matt. 20:25-26, GNB). It is not to be the way Christians are to relate to one another—including in marriage.

Even Christians, who are aware that they are to be mutually submissive to one another, sometimes lose sight of their calling to covenantal love. In the heat and frustration of the angry moment, they may try to defeat their partner. Winning, proving that I am right, that my position is best, or that I am completely blameless and whatever happened was all my partner's fault, becomes all-important. Partners who get caught up in the "I win, you lose" game often are trying to prove something to themselves as much as they are to their partner. If I do not like myself very much, or if I cannot accept the fact that I make mistakes, then winning becomes a way to say to myself and to the most important person in my life, "See, I'm OK; I'm right; I'm a good partner. Any problems we have can't be my fault."

When such hidden self-esteem issues are involved, the fuss can become much hotter and last much longer than the problem deserves. For example, Marge and Mac argued for four days over who carried the heaviest load of household responsibilities. The hot words exchanged were broken only by long silences in which they retreated to their corners of the house to gather more steam for the next round. Both wanted to be right and to prove the other wrong. To be right meant to be better than the other. Both wanted to blame the other for how tired and pressured they felt. Both would feel better about themselves if the other would express appreciation for them by saying "you're right." Unfortunately, since both needed it, neither was willing to give it to the other.

An issue like this can become like a whirlpool. Once you have been sucked in, it is terribly hard to get out. Many arguments in marriage, which seem to the casual observer to be over such petty things, wind up like this. We want so badly for our partner to respect us. We think the way to get this respect is always to be right. But to be right means that the other must be wrong. Couples caught in the anger that comes from seeking to get their needs met in all the wrong ways can and need to learn new ways to give and seek respect from one another.

When Anger Keeps Partners from Finding Creative Ways To Make Needed Changes

One of the most serious problems with anger is that it blocks partners' abilities to solve problems and make needed changes. It takes energy and creativity to solve many of the problems in marriage. Nothing blocks our ability to be creative like stress that comes from anger. The angrier we get, the less chance we have for coming out with a good, workable solution for the issue we face. Marge and Mac, for example, were caught in so much anger, stress, and frustration, that they could not even see how crazy their conflict had become. Their vision became narrowed to one option: proving one right and the other wrong. They could not see any other possibilities.

Helpful Hints for Dealing with Anger in Marriage

See Anger as a Powerful Tool for Truth

When Jesus overturned the tables and drove the money changers and the sacrificial animals out of the Temple, His goal was not to get the anger out of His system so that He would feel better. He was using His righteous anger to communicate to the Temple authorities a message from God—this is what God thinks about what is going on here. Anger can be a tool for truth or for evil. When it is used to confront the problems in a relationship, anger can be a constructive force. When it is used to exalt oneself and humiliate the other, it destroys.

Peace in a marriage which is based on one person giving up or on ignoring problems is no peace at all. We should not pretend everything is all right instead of openly facing the breach in a relationship. We are not to say, "'Peace, peace,' when there is no peace" (Jer. 6:14; 8:11; see also Ezek. 13:10-11,14-16). When God had a problem with Israel, God let them know it. When the psalmist had a problem with God, the psalmist boldly let God know it. It did not hurt the relationship; it strengthened it. Christian partners can and need to use anger as a tool for restoring and renewing their covenant.

Accept Grace from Partners

We don't have to be right to be justified, or to be perfect to be loved. Partners troubled with anger need to pause to ask themselves: What am I trying to do? Am I trying to work things out with my spouse, or am I trying to prove that I am a wonderful (right, long-suffering, mistreated, etc.) partner? If you are trying to prove something, anger is being used to bolster your self-esteem rather than to restore the relationship.

When anger is tied to self-esteem, we have not really taken to heart the good news of the gospel. I don't have to be right to be accepted by God. I do not have to be perfect to be loved by God. This is also true in marriage. If our partners love us, they will love us when we are wrong and imperfect. We need to learn to accept this love.

Learn New Skills for Handling Angry Feelings

The skills of sharing ourselves and listening to one another discussed in chapter 3 are perhaps the most important skills partners can use in handling anger. They are also the most difficult. It is hard to risk oneself by sharing thoughts and feelings when we are angry. It is much easier to lash out at or to blame the partner. It is hard to say, "I am angry because I was running late this morning and you left me the car without any gas. I just filled it up the day before yesterday, and I was counting my time to the last second. I don't want to have to fill up the car with gas after you have driven it, especially without any warning." It may be easier to say, "I am so angry with you. How could you be such a bubble brain! You *knew* I had to get to work early this morning, so you deliberately left me the car without any gas!" It is also hard to listen when we are angry. Usually, all we can think about is what we are feeling and how wronged we have been. It is hard to stop stewing inside long enough to see what happened from the partner's viewpoint.

Another skill that can be useful in handling anger, particularly if couples struggle with wanting to win or with giving anger a life of its own, is postponing talking about it. This does not mean long cold silences. It means deciding together to talk about it when we have both calmed down. If we tend toward violence when we are angry, we particularly need some time out before we begin talking. This time out is not simply an opportunity to escape the anger and think about something else. We need to think about what the problem really is and think through ways we can talk with our partner about it. We need to think of ways that will restore our relationship, not destroy it.

In preparing to express our anger, we also need to go back through the source of our anger. First, what is the *actual event* that set off our anger? It was the fact that "you were talking with a certain person." It was *not* that "you were flirting with a certain person." "Flirting" is the *interpretation* we gave to the event. That needs to be the next thing at which we look.

Second, we need to look at our interpretation of the event. What other possible interpretations could be given to the event? It helps to keep in our mind that we are angry not only because something has happened, but because of what we thought about what happened. We should remember that our thoughts are not fool proof.

Third, we need to reflect on what is going on in our *own bodies*. Are we under stress from other relationships? Are we tired? Are we worried about something else? Are we hungry? How much are we using anger at our spouse as a channel to spew out a lot of other tension?

We need to pray continuously about our anger. We need to ask God's help in being a faithful covenant partner, in being strong and taking seriously the problem that faces us. Also, we should ask for help in being loving and being mindful of our partners' needs.

Thinking through and praying through our anger can help

prepare us to talk with each other in ways that will turn anger into intimacy and conflict into creative change. In the beginning, it may even help us to spell out to our partner what we thought while we were alone. Tell your partner: this is what happened. This is how I interpreted it. This is how I felt (angry, frightened, sick at my stomach). Then say, "With God's help, I want to sort it out with you so that we can be stronger."

Make Contracts with One Another for Expressing and Living with Our Anger

In chapter 3, we talked about how couples can use contracts to get started in new patterns in their life together. Contracts work well as a way to start handling anger differently. For example, counselors often begin work with couples who have been violent with one another by having them agree that no one will hit anyone else for any reason. Some couples find it helpful to agree that they will take ten minutes to cool off before they talk about their anger. Some of the body tension can then subside. They can also think through and pray through what they want to do with their anger. Still other couples find that they have been too silent with their anger. They may want to start using words instead of cold silences or slammed doors. They may contract with one another to try to say, "I am angry because . . ." anytime they find themselves using one of the old patterns.

Every marriage is different, and every couple needs to work out their own way of handling anger that will build on their covenant with one another. Learning to handle anger and to make creative changes is much easier to write about than it is to do. Some couples may find the discussion in this and the previous chapter helpful in trying new patterns in their own relationship. Others may need the support of a trusted counselor or a group of other couples who can help them through the process of change. Many churches offer marriage enrichment seminars and groups as part of their family ministry. If you are interested in such a learning experience, talk with your pastor, another church staff member, or the family ministry department in your denomination's office.

5

How Can We Change
Our Sexual Relationship?

God created us as sexual beings, and the Bible celebrates the goodness of this creation. The Song of Solomon and a number of proverbs express the beauty and pleasure of our sexuality:

> Three things are too wonderful for me;
>   four I do not understand:
> the way of an eagle in the sky,
>   the way of a serpent on a rock,
> the way of a ship on the high seas,
>   and the way of a man with a maiden
>   (Prov. 30:18-19).

Sexual intimacy is a sign of what it means to be in covenant with one another as "one flesh" (Gen. 2:24). As covenant partners, each gives of self to the other; and each tunes in to the special needs and feelings of the other. The potential for conceiving new life through sexual intimacy points to what marriage partners can be and do together that neither could accomplish alone.

The sexual relationship between partners, however, can easily become a source of trouble. Fatigue, changing moods, and tension in other parts of our lives play havoc with our ability to relax and share sex in a playful and intimate way. Our feelings of masculinity or femininity, key parts of our self-esteem, can become like raw nerves when a problem turns up in our sex life. Problems are made worse because we do not give ourselves permission to talk about our sexuality with one another. This leaves room for lots of misunderstanding and gives our sex life more power over us than it would have if we could talk about it.

In addition, Christians often find sex to be a particularly touchy subject because we are not sure what we are supposed to think about it. For some, it is hard to shake the feeling that sex might be sinful. After all, we were taught to keep our sexual impulses in check before marriage. Suddenly, upon saying, "I do," what had been forbidden is now an obligation. It is also supposed to be a blessing. Yet there may be a nagging concern that sex even in marriage is in some way dirty, or that it distracts us from more spiritual activities. Some of these concerns come from misunderstandings of what the Bible says about sex.

A Biblical View of Sexuality

One of the passages that gives Christians problems in understanding the role of sexuality in marriage is found in 1 Corinthians 7. In verse 9, for example, Paul wrote that one should marry only if it is the only way to avoid the sin of fornication. In verses 33-34, he wrote that those who are unmarried are "anxious about the affairs of the Lord, how to be holy in body and spirit." The married, however, are anxious about worldly affairs, how to please their spouses. Did Paul mean that married people are not as holy as unmarried people because of their sexual activity?

Paul did think it best not to marry. But it was not because he thought it was better to keep oneself pure from sexual activity. Paul believed that the coming end of the age with all its tribulations required that Christians focus every ounce of energy on devotion to the Lord (vv. 29-31). There would be enough to worry about without having the burden of a family to care for during these troubled times. The married have natural obligations that can keep them from turning all their attention to the Lord (vv. 32-35). Paul also knew that marriage was part of this world; and this world, with all of its institutions, was passing away. Therefore, marriage is not the most important thing in life.

Although Paul recommended against marriage, he made it absolutely clear that there is nothing wrong with getting married or being married. He advised that it was best, in fact, for those who needed what marriage has to offer (1 Cor. 7:9,36-38; see also 1 Tim. 5:11-14). Paul personally chose celibacy (1 Cor. 7:7,32), but he did not suggest that to be married and sexually active is to be less holy or less spiritual. Paul was convinced that a celibate life was simpler: it is less anxious (v. 32), more ordered (v. 35), and happier (v. 40). He also made it clear that this was his opinion (vv. 7,26). Many Christians throughout the centuries have agreed with Paul. Other Christians, however, have found marriage to be less anxious, more ordered, and happier than living life alone. They have also found that with a Christian partner they can be as devoted to the Lord as those who are single.

Paul wrote in 1 Corinthians 7:

> Now concerning the matters about which you wrote. It is well for a man not to touch a woman. But because of the temptation to immorality, each man should have his own wife and each woman her own husband. The husband should give to his wife her conjugal rights, and likewise the wife to her husband. For the wife does not rule over her own body, but the husband does; likewise the husband does not rule over his own body, but the wife does. Do not refuse one another except perhaps by agreement for a season (vv. 1-5).

In verse 1, "to touch" is a polite way of saying "have sexual intercourse." Some translations mistakenly render it, "It is good for a man not to marry" (NIV). Paul was not talking about whether or not people should marry at this point, however. The issue was whether or not married people should have sex.

The problem is that this sounds like Paul is advising people to refrain from sex. But this is definitely not the case. He is probably dealing with a question raised by the Corinthians in their letter to him. Unfortunately for us, we do not have a copy of that letter to see what Paul was responding to specifically. Most scholars today believe that in 7:1, Paul was quoting from a statement made by some group in the Corinthian church. It would appear that someone at Corinth had been preaching that Christians ought to refrain from sexual activity—even if they were married! The Corinthians wrote to Paul to ask his advice on this matter. Paul quoted the opponents' slogan and then refuted it. Paul said instead that, if you are married, you are to be fully married. This means that one *owes* the partner a sexual relationship (vv. 3-5). The sexual aspect of marriage is not the *most* important part of marriage, but Paul recognized it is *an* important part. Just as celibacy or abstinence does not put one on a higher spiritual level, sexuality in marriage does not blemish one's spirituality. The opponents in Corinth probably thought it did. They thought they could be like angels. They not only wanted to speak the tongues of angels (1 Cor. 13:1), they wanted to become asexual like angels, who "neither marry nor are given in marriage" (Matt. 22:30).

Paul responded negatively to this so-called "spiritual" approach to marriage. It just leads to trouble. To try to be celibate within marriage will open up the temptation to satisfy one's sexual needs outside of marriage (1 Cor. 7:2). Paul believed that sex in marriage is not only all right, it is a right. In marriage, we owe one another a sexual relationship. Paul said that each partner "rules over" the body of the other (vv. 3-4). This does not mean we can demand anything from our partner. It means we cannot deny our sexual relationship on a personal whim, even for so-called spiritual reasons.

Paul did believe that times may arise in a marriage when partners will choose not to be sexually active. This may be because they carry a heavy burden and want to withdraw for a time of prayer. Paul insisted, however, that this must be by mutual agreement. One partner is not to withdraw independently from the other. Partners need to talk about their needs and agree together. Paul also insisted that this withdrawal is to have a time limit. Couples are not to see how long they can avoid having sex (v. 5). Again, Paul recognized that this would only lead to trouble.

Paul believed that sexual activity in marriage was normal. He also believed that there are times when we need to refrain from sexual activity. This does not make us any more spiritually "right" or "holy." Paul simply recognized that persons at times have needs that interfere with sexual feelings. But we need to share these needs with one another so that, whether we have sex or decide to refrain, we share in the shape our relationship takes. When this happens, our intimacy deepens, whether or not there is sexual activity. This is exactly the opposite of what happens when one partner becomes angry and resentful and sleeps on the sofa or forces the other to do so. It is also different from what happens when one endures silently the burdens from the marriage or fakes a headache or some other excuse in order to be left alone. How much better to face together the conflict, or a personal need for solitude, instead of using anger and deception to provide needed distance on occasion.

Paul was clear that the nature of the sexual relationship between married partners was to be holy. In 1 Thessalonians 4:3-5, he wrote:

> For this is the will of God, your sanctification: that you abstain from unchastity; that each one of you know how to take a wife for himself in holiness and honor, not in the passion of lust like heathen who do not know God.

A Christian marriage is not to be governed by lust. Lust does not mean sexual desire. Christians, if they are physically and emotionally healthy, have sexual desires. What is important is that these desires do not become twisted and misused. "Lust" means to treat the other as an object, a "thing." Lust uses the other selfishly for one's own pleasure without thought for the personhood or needs of the other. Loving and committed partners are not to treat one another like things to be used. We are to honor and treat the one with whom we have been joined in marriage as holy. The question Christians are to ask themselves is, "What can I *give* to my partner?" not "What can I *get* from my partner?" God intended that when marriage partners love one another sexually, they give something to one another. Therefore, expressing our sexuality should be something more than simply a way for us to procreate or to satisfy bodily desires. It is God's way for humans to join their very selves together (see 1 Cor. 6:16).

Our bodies are instruments that are to be used to glorify God (v. 20). One way that we do this is to communicate love, acceptance, and belonging through our sexual relationship with our married partner. Does having sex with one another "in holiness and honor" mean that sex is to be serious business? Should certain things be done or avoided to make sex holy? The Bible says nothing about this. "Holy" does not mean "solemn." Holy occasions can include quiet prayer and serious words, but they can also include laughter and joyful noises (see 2 Sam. 14—15). There is not one way to be holy. The joy of playfulness, of erotic sharing with one another, and of exploring together new ways of relating to one another sexually can be holy when we are sensitive to one another's needs.

Every marriage is unique, and the relationship between partners is to be based on the personhood of the partners. The sexual relationship of the marriage will reflect this uniqueness. The partners should not worry about fitting some pattern that they have read about or heard about as if it were ideal. What is good is that which brings intimacy and joy to the partners.

How our relationship compares with the sexual relationships of other marriages is not important. We can summarize, then, the role of sex in the lives of married Christians:

(1) Partners are to be active sexually (1 Cor. 7:1-2).

(2) Partners are to give themselves freely to one another. They are not to use sex as a weapon in conflict or as a reward to the partner for some good done (vv. 3-4).

(3) Partners may choose not to have sex for a time, but it is to be for a limited time. Partners are to talk first about this and come to an agreement. One cannot dictate to the other (v. 5).

(4) Partners are to treat one another with respect and be concerned about one another's needs as persons. They are not to treat one another as objects of pleasure (1 Thess. 4:3-8; 1 Pet. 3:7).

(5) Exploring new ways to express sexuality with one another can be holy and respectful when partners are sensitive to one another. There is no one way to express sexuality in marriage. It needs to reflect the uniqueness of the marital relationship.

(6) In the sexual sharing of marriage, partners need to give one another the message that they are loved, accepted, and belong to each other.

A couple's sex life reflects the health and strength of their relationship. If they love and respect one another, if they can communicate effectively with one another and resolve conflicts in ways that are mutually satisfying, their sexual relationship will be one of shared intimacy and pleasure. They will experience moments of disappointment, but couples should be able to bounce back and even laugh at themselves. They will also experience periods of sexual inactivity, but these will be balanced by times of greater intimacy and sexual activity. Partners in healthy, mature marriages do not worry about whether or not their sex life is above average or below average when compared to other couples. They concern themselves instead with the role sex needs to have in their own unique relationship.

This is the ideal of what the sexual relationship of married couples should be like. Let us now look at some of the troubles couples have in their sexual lives with one another.

Sexual Troubles in Marriage

In troubled marriages, sex often becomes yet another battleground. It can mirror the problems couples experience in other aspects of their relationship. Some troubled couples report that they have a wonderful sexual relationship in spite of their other miseries. Indeed, some couples find that their sexual intimacy is a strength that helps them weather the other storms in their relationship. For most couples, however, their sex life is the first place where trouble crops up. This is because sex requires partners to communicate with one another and to risk themselves with one another more than in any other area of marriage. We will discuss some common troubles partners experience in their sexual relationship.

Couples Expect Their Marriage to Be Like the Movies

In television show, movies, and novels, sex is the major aspect of the relationship between a man and a woman. Both men and women are judged by their ability as sexual partners. Our culture emphasizes being skillful at sex. More is believed to be better. The more often a couple has sexual intercourse the better the sex is supposed to be. Reaching climax at the same time is considered the ideal, even though few couples actually are able to do this.

As a result of these popular beliefs, couples may feel uncertain about their own sexual relationship. They may worry if the sex in their marriage is "good enough." Each may wonder if the other is truly satisfied, especially if their sexual relationship does not seem to measure up to the myths of our society. They may find themselves keeping a mental notebook on how many times each week or month they have intercourse, to see if they are "normal" or not. The "goodness" of their marriage and the self-worth of each as a man and as a woman rests on how much their sex life looks like or is better than everybody else's.

Instead of being a time of playful sharing and intimacy, the sexual relationship becomes work, a place to prove that me and my marriage are above average (Lewis & Brissett, 1977). Instead of taking risks with one another, partners may try to impress each other. Instead of sharing and enjoying the pleasure of each other's embrace, partners mentally stand back and watch and grade their own performance (Masters & Johnson, 1966).

Focusing on how well we are doing leads to anxiety—"Are we doing Ok?" "Does she like what I am doing?" "What does he think of me?" Anxiety and sexual responsiveness do not mix. The more anxious one is, the less sexually responsive one becomes. Anxiety may make it difficult for a woman to respond to her husband. It may cause a man to reach orgasm too soon to meet either his or his partner's needs. Such occasional troubles are normal; but if the partners are already anxious about their performance, their anxiety may increase even more. This will make it more likely that the trouble will occur again. A vicious circle begins—a sexual problem leads to anxiety about performance—which leads to the problem occurring again—which leads to more anxiety. Soon the couple may find themselves struggling with a problem in their sexual relationship that they cannot deal with without professional assistance.

The problem may not get bad enough for the couple to seek help. It may simply smolder and create distance and perhaps even dishonesty between partners. Dennis worried because Christy did not have an orgasm during intercourse. Giving Christy a satisfying sexual experience became work for Dennis. He decided that he did not measure up as a sexual partner. He became detached during their lovemaking, trying to distract himself with other thoughts in order to delay his own orgasm.

Christy, on the other hand, sensed how important it was to Dennis for her to reach orgasm during intercourse. Then she sensed that he was becoming distant during their lovemaking. She thought that he was bored and unhappy with her as a sexual partner. She decided one evening to pretend to have an orgasm during intercourse. Dennis was so pleased that she felt from then on that she needed to fake orgasm in order to please him.

Instead of accepting each other, both partners pushed each other into a dishonest game of pretend. Instead of playfully exploring ways they can meet each other's needs, they tried to copy what they think sex is "supposed" to be like. Instead of being in touch with themselves and with each other, they feel separated from their own feelings and anxious about how well they are doing.

Christy and Dennis have missed what God intended sexuality in marriage to be. They thought they were trying to be sensitive and respectful of one another's needs: Dennis was trying to be the good husband and meet his wife's needs, and Christy was trying to bolster her husband's feelings of manhood. They were trying to be good sexual partners according to what they had heard or read. But they failed to hear or read one another. What is good sex for Christy and Dennis is that which brings them pleasure as individuals and intimacy as a couple. Pleasure includes the joy in their sharing as a couple, and the renewal of their covenant with one another. None of this will come about with Dennis trying to distract himself or with Christy's faking.

Couples Find It Hard to Be Playful

So much of our life together as a couple is work. We parent our children, we run a household, we try to coordinate our jobs and other commitments, and we care for one another and for other family members. Sex, however, was created to be playful. Play is activity that we engage in because it brings us pleasure and joy, and not necessarily because it accomplishes some task. Pleasure is just as much a part of our God-created sexuality as is the potential for conceiving children. Of all of our bodily functions, sex brings the most pleasure. Our brains are wired in such a way that sex brings feelings of love and affection as well as pleasure (Kaplan, 1974). God made us sexual not only to conceive children, but also to enjoy one another, and through that enjoyment, to deepen our love and affection for one another. God could have chosen another way to continue the human race. Instead, God chose to make the conception of children part of a larger creative process. We not only can create children in our sexual relationship, we can also create and deepen the companionship and intimacy of our marriage covenant with one another.

The playfulness of sex may get lost, however, in the pressures of a troubled marriage. Couples who lead highly stressful lives may find it difficult to carve out time in which they can relax together and allow the tension of their daily life to drain away. Instead, their sexual relationship may seem as driven and tense as the rest of their lives. Sex is no longer playful; it is yet another task to be accomplished.

Couples' Values and Beliefs About Sex and Intimacy Are Different

We bring with us into marriage not only the ideals and values of our culture, but also the ideals and values of our families. We also bring to marriage our own earlier sexual experiences, whatever they may have been. The values and experiences one partner brings to a marriage may be quite different from what the other brings.

Wife's family, for example, may have never talked about sex. What she knows she learned at school and in the hushed talk of girl friends at slumber parties. Her parents may have had a troubled marriage. She never saw them express any affection for one another, and they slept in separate bedrooms. She cannot imagine how she was ever conceived.

Husband, on the other hand, may come from a family that was very open about sexuality. Both of his parents talked with him about his own sexual development and the joys and responsibilities of sex. He learned from them that sex is a playful and important part of marriage. His parents often kissed and embraced in front of the children. His father often patted his wife's hip playfully, which she greeted with an affectionate smile. The children enjoyed the outward signs of their parents' attraction for one another.

As you can imagine, this couple brings to marriage quite different values and beliefs about the role of sex in marriage. Although Wife wants her marriage to be very different from her parents', she still finds it hard to accept the playful, open attitude toward sex that Husband has. Husband is disappointed and hurt by what seems to him to be her cold response to his affection. She gets angry when he pats her or shows his love in other ways in the presence of others. This couple needs to share with one another their different views about sex and experiences in their families. This will help them with their feelings of being misunderstood. If they stay open and accepting of one another and their differences, they can work out patterns in their relationship over time that both find satisfying.

Some couples have more serious differences with which they must deal. One or both may have had previous sexual experiences that make it difficult to risk and share openly in their sexual relationship. Adults who were victims of incest as children or who were molested or raped either as children or as adults may have real difficulty allowing themselves to risk being vulnerable to a sexual partner, even in the safety of marriage. This may be the case when they do not remember the experience or even when they think that they have overcome it. Partners may have been shamed during their adolescence about their sexual development by parents or others. Partners may also have had troublesome sexual experiences as adults which have left scars of embarrassment or anxiety about their sexuality.

Partners who have had such experiences may need help so that they are better able to risk and be intimate with their spouses. Groups such as Adults Molested as Children and Parents United can be very helpful, as can professional counseling. Your local community mental health center or Christian counseling center can put you in touch with a local chapter of these self-help organizations or a professional competent to deal with sexual problems in marriage. Most of all, one needs the loving acceptance and support of a patient partner.

Couples Have Difficulty Sharing Their Needs and Secret Desires

Troubled couples often believe that their partners ought to know what they are thinking. They think that they should not have to talk about sex: "If she loved me, she would know what I want"; "If he loved me, he would know what pleases me and what irritates me." For some reason, some couples believe that talking about it "ruins it." Just because you love someone does not mean that you also have a special ability to read the other's mind. Love just gives partners the *desire* to understand each other. The knowing must come through sharing.

Talking about sexual desires and fantasies can be very risky business. "What will she think if I tell her that I would really like to take a blanket out to the woods and make love to her there?" "What will he think if I suggest we try a different position for intercourse?" Each may be afraid the other will laugh or be disgusted by what they want, and so they never find out.

Such intimate sharing requires a relationship in which each feels the respect of the other. Partners learn to trust that the other will not hurt or embarrass them from the way they work through their anger and the way they make decisions. The husband who says to his wife in a morning argument, "How can you think that? You are such an idiot! I don't know where you get your crazy ideas!" should not expect his wife to risk sharing her most secret thoughts and desires in their lovemaking that evening. The wife who reacts to her husband's latest plans for the family vacation with, "That's the dumbest thing I've ever heard!" should not expect him to unveil his innermost feelings.

Partners' Needs Are Different

Partners not only begin their marriage with different values and beliefs about sex, but with different needs as well. For example, a male's sexual interests and responsiveness peak in his late teens and early twenties. After this they slowly decline. A female's sexual interest and responsiveness may not peak until her thirties. Young husbands, therefore, may be much more interested in sexual intimacy than their wives. Later in their marriage, the wives' interests may exceed that of their husbands' (Masters & Johnson, 1966). This is based on the "average" husband and wife, and no one is average! Different people have different levels of sexual interest and responsiveness, and the individual needs of the partners in a marriage are far more important than any "average." The point is that husbands and wives may have different needs at different times in their lives.

Partners may also find that their sexual lives are affected by other factors. Certain illnesses and chronic diseases may lessen sexual interest or limit the ability to be involved sexually. Chronic pain of any kind may dull the ability of partners to respond sexually to one another. Even if the illness itself does not affect the partner's sex drive, many medications lessen sexual interest or the physical ability to respond to one another.

Nothing in the aging process itself need hinder the sexuality of partners who love one another and want to remain sexually active. Many couples remain sexually intimate with one another into their eighties and beyond. Like other body processes, the phases of sexual excitement and response to one another slow with age. Many of the diseases that come with aging may indeed create sexual problems. This can also create frustration. It is only made worse when partners do not understand the causes of the problem and blame one another. This adds a sense of failure, hurt, and misunderstanding to the sexual trouble.

When couples have very different needs and the possibility of a physical cause to the trouble is present, they need to talk with a physician. If medicine is the cause of the problem, sometimes the medicine can be changed. Many of the physical ailments that create sexual problems can be treated. Most important, a couple should tackle the problem they face *together* and not allow it to become a wedge that separates them.

Couples Limit Intimacy in Their Relationship to Sex

Our sexual organs are only 1 percent of our bodies, and sex usually comprises only about 1 percent of our relationship with each other (Pittman, 1984). In a troubled marriage, however, sex may be the only kind of intimacy that couples share. Almost always, this limited kind of intimacy does not meet the partners' needs. A sense of intimacy is created when we feel we belong to one another, support one another, and like one another. Intimacy also comes from talking about all the important and unimportant things that fill our lives (Tolstedt & Stokes, 1983). Marriage is far more than sex. If sex, even intimate, loving sex, is all that a couple shares, one or both partners will soon begin to feel lonely and perhaps even used. Sex may become simply a way to release sexual tension. It does not build the covenant between the partners.

Couples Use Sex As a Reward or As a Weapon

Often in a troubled marriage, sex may become a weapon in the combat between the partners. Denying the partner sexual intimacy may be used to punish the partner for some imagined wrong or to communicate anger. Even in healthy marriages, conflict may keep spouses from being interested in sexual intimacy with one another. If that becomes a regular pattern, the marriage itself is troubled.

The sexual relationship can be a good litmus test to see how healthy a marriage is. Couples can see how flexible and open to change they are by seeing the degree to which their roles in their sexual relationship are flexible. Can both husband and wife, for instance, make the first move toward sexual intimacy? Can they relate differently at different times, with one being more active at one time and the other at another? Can their sexual intimacy change to fit their needs, from a brief, loving encounter in the middle of the night to a playful, longer time of intimacy on a Saturday morning?

Troubled couples often have set patterns that do not change. One partner always begins the sexual intimacy and almost always in the same way. Like many of the other patterns in the marriage, their sexual relationship is a well-worn habit. Even though both may feel bored and long for creative change in their relationship, any change that takes place seems more upsetting than exciting.

Ways to Make Changes

Despite the fact that the sexual relationship between partners seems more delicate than other parts of a marriage, the ways to go about making changes differ very little from making changes in any other marital pattern. Listening and understanding, giving support and respect, tackling problems together instead of trying to blame each other, even using contracts and other methods of making change discussed in chapters 2 and 3 are all helpful. In addition, some other suggestions may be useful in creating change in a sexual relationship.

Look Together at Sexual Expectations

Look together at what we expect from our sexual relationship, our values and beliefs about sexuality, and our own individual needs. One of the hardest things for many couples to do is simply to talk about their sexual relationship. Spouses may begin by reading something together, such as this chapter, and talking about their thoughts and feelings about what they read. An excellent time to read and talk is on a car trip. One can read while the other drives, and there is plenty of time to share thoughts and feelings.

Another helpful way to begin talking about sex with one another is to share our individual sexual histories, and then build toward talking about our current sexual relationship. What was the sexual relationship of your parents like? What did they tell you about sex? Where else did you learn about sex? What were you told, and what did you think about it? Were there any experiences you had as a child, teenager, or adult that you think have affected your thoughts and feelings about sex that you want to share with your partner? What did you think sex would be like when you got married? What were your hopes? What do you like best about your sexual relationship now? What would you like to change about *your* (not your partner's!) part in your sexual relationship?

Make a Contract to Try Something Different in Your Sexual Relationship

If the sexual relationship seems more like a habit than a time of intimacy, *any* change may help shake loose your patterns of relating and help get you moving toward the way you would like your relationship to be. Contracts can be useful tools even in our sexual relationship to get change started. Couples who have highly stressful lives, for example, may find that the only way they can make time for sexual intimacy is to make a contract for it. They set a time on the calendar, an "appointment" with one another. What they do with that time, whether they take a walk or a drive, talk over a cup of coffee or make love, is up to how they happen to feel at the time and what they need from one another. The important thing is that they have made the time available.

Struggling with a different kind of problem, Jeff and Suzanne felt frustrated because their relationship seemed stuck in the same old pattern. In order to shake loose of their boredom, they decided that they would take turns for four weeks planning a sexual experience that was somehow different from their old pattern. They agreed to surprise each other. They both agreed to go along with the other unless they were *very* uncomfortable with the plan. (They were wise enough to know that any change was going to be somewhat uncomfortable.) The first week, Jeff took Suzanne for a long evening drive and parked the car, where they talked and kissed and shared as they had done before they were married. The second week, Suzanne, wrapped in a bath towel, met Jeff at the door when he came home from work and invited him to take a bath with her. They found these times very enjoyable. The third and fourth weeks were not very "successful." Jeff took Suzanne and a blanket out to the backyard one night during the third week, but they were both too worried about being seen by the neighbors to enjoy themselves. Despite the fact that the last times were not as much fun as the first, Suzanne and Jeff were able to have a good laugh at themselves. They did not continue their contract after the fourth week, but their sexual relationship was definitely improved. They both felt free to be more creative in their sexual relationship with one another.

Seek Help When You Need It

Have you ever been swimming under the water and tried to see what is happening above the water? If you have, you know that you cannot see very well. What you may see is only a blur. Sometimes when we are in the midst of a troubled marriage, and particularly when our sexual relationship is troubled, it is impossible for us to see out. Our self-esteem and our feelings keep us from seeing possibilities "out there" that can make a difference in our marriage. Everything is a blur. Professional helpers often can provide a different viewpoint because they are outside the marriage. They can point out new possibilities and new ways of viewing our troubles that give us new choices about how to live faithfully and joyfully together.

Being willing to get this help may also take each partner supporting the other. Although society sees counseling more positively today than in the past, many still view it negatively. The couple who recognizes the need for counseling will also need to understand the benefits. Getting a troubled marriage back on track is worth bucking whatever negative views society may place in the way.

6

How Can We Cope When Pressed on Every Side?

Many couples with troubled marriages might well have satisfying, healthy marriages if they were not overwhelmed by crises that stem from sources other than their relationship with one another. Even in the healthiest of marriages, couples can experience a crisis in their relationship because of the difficulties they face in the world around them.

Three aspects of a couple's world were described in chapter 1 as possible sources of trouble: their physical context (their home, community, climate, weather, etc.), their interpersonal context (children, parents, friends, neighbors, workmates, etc.), and their context of cultural ideas and beliefs (newspapers, televisions, magazines, radio). We touched on some of the problems which cultural ideas and beliefs can create when we talked in chapter 2 about the expectations we hold for marriage, and in chapter 5 when we talked about our culture's views on sexuality. In this chapter, we will focus primarily on the interpersonal contexts of couples that often have a major impact on their marriages. These infer personal contexts made up of parents and other family members, the world of work, church, friends, and children. We will also take a look at the relationship of couples with their physical world.

Parents and Extended Family

Parents and other extended family can create strain in a marriage in any number of ways. "Extended family" are those

117

related by blood and marriage except one's own spouse and children living in the same house. Extended family members may be parents, grandparents, aunts and uncles, cousins, nieces and nephews, grandchildren, and step relatives. Sometimes these extended family members create strife in a marriage. Perhaps they did not approve of the marriage in the first place. Or their values and beliefs may differ from those of the spouse marrying into the family. Sometimes these differences surface at a family gathering. When one husband went with his wife to her family's annual Thanksgiving dinner reunion, for example, his remarks about the need for more peacemaking in the world ran head-on into the values of the wife's favorite uncle who is a career military man. A heated argument followed that resulted in strained family relationships. The wife is embarrassed and angry; the husband never wants to see her family again.

A parent may have difficulty accepting that a child has grown up, moved away from home, and now shares his or her heart with someone else. The new spouse is a direct threat to the parent's desire to continue to be the "special one" in the adult child's life. Stress caused by in-law problems in young marriages are not uncommon. The countless jokes about mothers-in-law reflect that we are all aware of the problems that can arise.

In one marriage, Husband stopped at his mother's house each day after work. He did small chores for her, and she prepared his supper. After supper, he headed home to his young wife. During the first year of their marriage, the wife did not mind this. She was working and did not have to fix dinner when she got home. After fourteen months of marriage, however, their first child was born. Things changed. The wife quit working to stay home with the new baby. The pattern that had worked up to that point became a serious problem. After spending the day with an infant, the wife looked forward to her husband's return. This would give her both adult company as well as the chance to let someone else help with the care of the baby for awhile. Her anger at both her husband and mother-in-law flared when neither seemed to recognize a need for a change in their established pattern.

Parents are not the only ones who can interfere in a marriage. Many couples whose children have left home are finding their empty nests full again as children return home for a time. This is sometimes a less than welcome arrangement. Parents have readjusted to their life as a couple alone. Having grown children in the house again with different schedules, interests, and friends can create serious conflict between partners as they disagree over how to respond to the situation.

Coping with the illness or problems of parents or other extended family also can create stress in a marriage. The divorce of parents married thirty years or more, the need of a relative to have expensive nursing care, the alcoholism of a parent, or the lay-off of a brother with a young family can have a negative impact on a marriage. When a couple is comfortable with their marriage, they can handle most family stresses creatively. If the marriage is already under stress and crises arise on several fronts, trouble becomes likely. The crises pile up and the stress multiplies. This leaves the couple less and less able to respond with energy and creativity to the demands placed on them.

The World of Work

Most Americans, if asked what the major source of stress in their lives is, will likely respond, "my work." The major portion of our adult lives is spent working. We spend more waking time at work than with our spouses. Yet partners may not even talk about their work with one another, fearing that the other will be bored or will not understand. Or, they may want to leave work at the office and preserve the home as an island away from the pressures of the business world.

Work may create special stresses in the lives of partners. For example, a counselor met with a couple who complained about poor communication and frequent conflict that verged on violence. It was only after spending two hours with them that the counselor learned that one worked the 8 AM to 5 PM shift; the other worked the 3 PM to 11 PM shift. The only time they had together to talk, work through conflict, or simply be together had to be taken from the sleep time of one or the other. No wonder they were having communication problems!

For some people, work involves not only the forty hours they put in at the office, but also requires frequent or lengthy travel, overtime, bringing work home, or expectations for business entertainment. Some partners may enjoy the added demands of traveling because it gives them the chance to be alone. They may enjoy socializing with one another's business associates. For others, however, these added work demands may be sources of stress.

One of the hardest kinds of stress is that which requires partners to change their daily patterns in dramatic ways. For example, military personnel or spouses who commute to other cities to work may be away from home for long periods of time. Partners adjust to living independently of one another, making decisions and living day in and day out almost as single persons. Then, they are thrown together for a weekend or a longer period of time in which they expect themselves to "act married" and depend on one another in ways that they cannot during their separations. Conflict may result.

Unemployment, of course, creates a special kind of stress in marriage. Not only does the sudden loss of income create hardship, but the daily patterns of living are totally disrupted at a time that partners may not be able to cope easily with such change. For example, a husband who has been going to work early and getting home late is now home all day, while his wife continues her job. Child care, cooking, housework, and other tasks that have been shared or have been the responsibility of his wife suddenly become his responsibility while she works longer hours to support the family. These are perhaps new tasks for him, and learning new tasks when one is anxious and depressed is extremely difficult. The potential for marital turmoil builds. Quarreling increases as partners try to adjust their spending habits and their patterns of living to a much reduced income. Roles change, and with them, the normal ways of making decisions and keeping life running smoothly. According to research, unemployment results in marital stress that can lead to poorer communication, confusion in defining roles with one another, and an increase in violence (Larson, 1984; and Voydanoff, 1983).

Children

Perhaps nothing brings greater joy or stress to a marriage than the birthing and rearing of children. We normally expect that children will bring couples closer together and give their relationship purpose and meaning. Research, however, has found that just the opposite is true. Couples with children report far less satisfaction and intimacy in their marriages than childless couples. Marital happiness is greater before children are born and after they leave home (Campbell, Converse, & Rogers, 1976; Glenn & Weaver, 1978; Luckey & Bain, 1970; Renne, 1970; Rollins & Galligan, 1978; Russell, 1974; Ryder, 1973; Spanier, Lewis, & Cole, 1975). This is particularly true for couples who are already experiencing stress in their marriage before children are born. Couples who have satisfying marriages experience less stress and negative change in their relationship with the birth of a child than those who are troubled (Harriman, 1986).

Several reasons may account for this. First, like unemployment, birthing and rearing children require partners to change their patterns of living together. Roles have to change. If a couple's patterns are flexible, making such changes may not be too difficult. If a couple has become stuck in deep ruts, needed changes may create a great deal of stress.

Although it takes two people to conceive a child, rearing a child does not require the joint effort of both parents. The rearing of children is still primarily the mother's responsibility in most families, although Dad gives some help. Dad usually feels the increased responsibility for providing for his growing family and may throw himself more into his work. The mom who is not working outside the home is absorbed in the twenty-four-hour care of growing children. As a result, a couple may find themselves going off in different directions, even if both are employed. This is a second reason that marriages experience more stress after children are born. Instead of a joint effort, they may choose to "divide and conquer." Husband may say, "You raise the kids, and I'll provide the money." When both parents are working, they may feel forced to divide up the home and child-care responsibilities. The birth of a child can give a couple a shared purpose and added meaning to their life together. But a child is also an added drain on their resources.

Parents soon discover that children are not lumps of clay that parents can mold according to their wishes. Children come into the world with their own personalities and quirks. They may develop problems that in the beginning have little to do with how their parents nurture and guide them. For example, a child may be hyperactive and aggressive. This may lead to significant difficulties in school. The root of the problem may be in some physical disorder. Parents who seek to give such a child the large amounts of love and the firm guidance that is necessary will have their hands full. They may experience a great deal of stress in their relationship as they try to make sense of their child's difficulties and cope with them. In their worry about their child, and in the added stress they experience, parents may blame themselves or each other.

Many parents of teenagers experience the stress of trying to cope with the strong influences of other adolescents toward drug use. Teenagers who become involved with drugs or alcohol may or may not have done so if their parents had been more or less controlling, or more or less damanding in what they expected of their child, or just simply more loving. Parents sometimes have to muddle through the raising of teenagers the best they can. The stress from this can give the marital relationship a beating. They may experience pain and blame each other for some imagined shortcoming that caused all of the problems. They may disagree about how to respond to their child and how to resolve the problem. They are anxious and worried; and, as we have noted before, high anxiety makes it almost impossible to respond creatively and thoughtfully to stress.

The Physical Context

The physical context in which a couple lives may also create stress.

Money

Some couples do not enjoy spending the time and energy that is required to manage and care for a household. With enough money, they can hire others to do conflict-ridden household maintenance tasks such as household repairs and cleaning. They can pay someone to provide child care. They can purchase two cars so that they do not have to coordinate their schedules.

Most couples, however, do not have the luxury of paying to have someone else take care of the responsibilities that create stress for them. In fact, many couples have to struggle with not having enough money even for the necessities. Partners have to stretch themselves over the many demands of a family with no resources to draw on beyond one another. Budgeting money and time requires careful coordination, which often can itself become a source of stress.

The stress of not enough money is made worse for the troubled couple by the fact that they live in an affluent society. They see the so-called ideal life-style of the upper middle class on television. But most will never have enough money to live the way characters do on TV. Problems arise when they find this life-style alluring and want to imitate it. This can lead to frustration. It can also lead to stress when a couple tries to live beyond their means. When money problems occur, it is easy to blame things on one another. The result is that they add marital troubles to the financial problems.

Privacy and Togetherness

Stress can be created by the physical space we share. Couples need space where they can have privacy together away from children and others in the family. Partners also need private space that even their spouses respect—a desk top, a special chair, a closet, or, for those who can afford it, a room in the house that they can call "mine." When no boundaries exist for private space, stress builds and the probability of anger and conflict rises. A family with three children living in a two-bedroom apartment can expect daily life to be hectic and stressful.

Weather, Climate, and Seasons

Our feelings are dramatically affected by the season of the

year and the climate. These feelings often ripple through the marriage. For example, family violence is known to increase when weather forces families to stay inside the house together. Excessive heat also causes increased family squabbles. Rain for weeks on end can lead to grumpiness and depression. Coping with natural disasters such as a fire in the home, storm damage, floods, and so on, may create enormous stress in individual partners and chaos in a marriage (Smith, 1983).

Usually, such stresses as drippy weather, cramped living quarters, or an empty bank account do not in themselves wreck a marriage. But they may create a climate of chronic stress and tension, so that spouses are more easily angered, and minor problems become blown out of proportion. At times, such additional stresses can be the last straw for a marriage already burdened down by crisis.

Ways We Ease Our Burdens

Turn Strain into a Shared Challenge

For a number of years, we have been told that stress of any kind does all kinds of bad things to us physically and emotionally. Everything from ulcers to divorce has been blamed on stress. Research on stress and crises, particularly crises in families, has shown that it is not simply stress that creates these problems. The meaning we give to the stress is a key factor (McCubbin & Patterson, 1983). This should sound familiar. In chapter 4, we pointed out how important the meaning we give to an event is in how we experience anger. It is not just the event that creates the stress, but how we interpret it. What may be the last straw for one couple, a stress beyond their ability to cope, may be an intimacy-building challenge for another couple.

There are three factors which create the kind of stress that often lead to problems for us individually and in our marriages. First, *we are not prepared for the stress.* It comes without warning. Not only does it seem to come out of the blue, but we also may have no prior experience to help us know how to handle it. We may not know anyone else who has experienced this kind of stress. For example, a couple who learns that their twenty-one-year-old son has AIDS will experience a great amount of stress. They are caught unprepared and probably do not know anyone else who has had to cope with this tragedy.

If there were some way to know beforehand what trials will face us, we could begin to prepare ourselves. This would help us face the stress before us constructively. This is usually impossible. If we can link up with others who have had the same kinds of experiences we are now facing, however, we may learn from them and can then feel less alone in the midst of a crisis.

Second, *we cannot make sense out of the crisis.*—It is normal when troubles come our way to ask ourselves, "Why should this be happening to us?" The answers to questions like these are seldom simple, if there even is an answer in this life. Things happen that are beyond our finite comprehension. The serious illness, death, or injury of one's child is perhaps the most difficult event with which a couple ever has to cope. In the midst of grief, these things simply do not seem to make any sense. Why should our child have to suffer? Why should *any* child suffer?

If our suffering or burden seems to have some purpose that we can identify, it is easier to bear. A fifty-five-year-old executive who is fired with no justifiable reason may sink into a depression and even think about suicide. He can make no sense out of why he devoted himself to a company that now simply ditches him. His life of service is considered by the powers that be to be inconsequential. His entire career seems to have been meaningless. He may believe he is a victim of age discrimination. The company can get out of paying his high salary and his future pension by hiring a younger replacement at far less cost. If he decides to fight for his own job and for the jobs of others in the company who are similarly threatened, his depression may lift. His burden now has a meaning. Through his experience and fight, he may be able to make a difference for others. The company will have to deal justly with employees in the future.

A mother whose young child has been killed by a drunk driver can make no sense of why this happened. She can replay the events over and over in her mind but the ending comes out the same. Her little child is dead. If that mother decides to fight in the legislature for stricter laws against drunk driving, the death of her child may take on a new meaning. Her persistence may prevent another child from becoming a victim of a drunk driver and an irresponsible host or tavern who allows a drunk to get behind the wheel.

Third, *we have no control over what is happening to us.*— One couple may choose to live without any luxuries because they have decided to give most of what they have to a mission cause. Another couple lives without any luxuries because they can only find part-time work at minimum wage. Which marriage experiences more stress? The couple that lives in poverty because they have no choice will feel the burden of their lack much more heavily than the couple who willingly chose their life-style.

We usually do not choose the struggles life tosses our way. A spouse develops a painful, chronic health condition; the death of a father leaves a widowed mother dependent on a young couple for support; a husband is laid off from work. Spouses do not choose these stresses in their shared life. Yet, they can make choices about how they will handle the stress, about how they will order their life around it, about what meaning they will give it. The vision of their calling as partners may give them the grace to accept and the willingness to embrace that which comes their way. They may then be able to give it meaning where others in the same circumstances would see none.

One of our favorite books that gives a picture of how this can happen in a marriage is entitled *Bethy and the Mouse* (Bakely, 1985). It is the diary of a father who struggles to cope with and make sense out of having two handicapped children. The first child was born with an abnormally small brain, probably because the mother suffered from food posioning during her pregnancy. He died when he was five. The second child, a daughter, was born years later with Down's syndrome. When she was born, the couple was already raising five other children. The husband's mother, who had serious health problems, was also living with them. In the beginning, this couple was not prepared for what they had to face in the birth of these children nor did they know others who struggled with similar family crises. The suffering of their children seemed meaningless. These crises were certainly not something they had chosen. They struggled to understand the meaning in this tragedy:

> "Why God? What in the world is the matter with you? What is there that gives you jollies in creating partial people? Why? Did you think things were getting too easy for us? Why do you want us to spend the rest of our years explaining, training, sheltering, carrying our last child?" (pp. 7-8).

In the midst of this crisis, however, this couple began to create answers for themselves with God's help. First, they sought other families who had similar experiences. They found professionals from whom they could learn how to cope with their special struggles and who could give their children the special education and medical care they needed. Second, they tried to find meaning in what seemed so meaningless. Through their prayers, and in their questioning, this couple found answers and special meaning in the lives of the children with which God had entrusted them. The father wrote:

> There are lots of Bethanys and Matthews in this world. We need them. They seem to bring out such good things in us, once we get to know them. They give us a special quality in our lives. They draw us out of our selfishness. They inspire us. They give us much more than they take. This world would lose so much without them (Bakely, 1985, p. XII).

In the end, what no parents ever would have chosen for themselves this couple embraced. The special needs of their children no longer were a burden but became a shared purpose and meaning for their lives. They also used their experiences to help others facing similar crises. Their writing about their experiences serves as inspiration to those who work with children with special needs and their families. This couple turned heartache into a shared challenge that provided purpose and meaning to their marriage covenant.

Develop Friends and Family Relationships

Develop friends and family relationships which provide love, care, and support during good times as well as times of trouble. The world around a couple can create stress and crisis for their marriage. But it can also provide support when stress threatens to pull a marriage apart. Research studies have shown that families who are the most troubled and in danger of blowing apart through divorce, violence, or physical or emotional illness are those who are most alone. They lack close friends and family (Anderson, 1982; Garland, 1987; Gray and others, 1979; Kotelchuck, 1982; McCubbin and Patterson, 1983; and Newberger and others, 1977).

Troubled marriages often scare away friends and extended

family. Those persons who could surround the couple with support may not know how to help. Or, they may have tried to help but were overwhelmed by the troubles. Couples with many problems often have so many needs that they cannot meet for themselves that they wear out friends and other family who try to help fill in the gaps. Relationships with others consist mostly of taking and little giving. Friendships, and even extended family relationships, need to be two-way streets. Persons with marital problems may want to talk endlessly about their troubles to the people who love them. But they may show little interest in listening to those who listen to them.

For example, a couple may be consumed with trying to cope with one partner's serious illness. They have to deal with massive changes in their finances and their daily lives. Their feelings are tied in knots as they try to sort out what is happening to them. Friends and family may rally around to provide meals, child care, and personal support for a time. But they may begin to feel that nothing they do is enough.

After several weeks of friends and families carrying in meals, the couple may hint that they are tired of casseroles and want something more varied. When friends and family deliver meals or pick up the children, they are met with a long tale of woe that they have heard again and again. They may even sense that the couple has come to depend on all the help they are getting and are not trying to make reasonable changes that will enable them to take over some of their own care. After awhile, friends who are tired from cooking extra meals and caring for extra children on top of the demands of their own families may drift away and leave the couple alone with their struggle.

Research also indicates that isolation may come first, and then comes the stressful event in a family's life. For example, couples who pull away from others or who live isolated lives are more likely to have marriage problems, including problems in communication, as well as physical and emotional problems in one or both partners. A prime time for such troubles to develop is right after a move to another town. Suddenly, a couple finds themselves all alone in a strange community. During such a period of isolation, illness, emotional upset, family troubles are more likely to crop up than when a couple is nestled in a web of supportive friends and family. Troubles may cause isolation. But it is also the case that isolation can cause troubles (Pilisuk & Parks, 1983)!

Troubled couples, therefore, need to pay attention to the community of support they have around them. People need to feel connected in some way to a number of other persons. No one person, not even the most wonderful of marital partners, can meet all of one's needs. And one person cannot be the receiver of all that one has to give. We need others who support us and care for us. We also need, in turn, to support and care for others.

Families.—In our mobile society, we may live far from our families. Even when we live in the same town, people are often so busy that they do not spend much time with their extended family. Many in our society feel that independence is so important that they do not wish to spend time regularly with their families. Some may worry that their family may interfere in some unhealthy way in their marriage. To cut off involvement with our extended families because they are not perfect, because conflict might arise, or because our values and beliefs are different is to cut ourselves off from one of the most important sources of strength and avenues for service that we have in life.

Ironically, if we cut off extended family relationships, it may give our families even more control over us in the long run than if we worked through the conflict with them the best that we could. We remain a part of our family, even if we choose to become "inactive members." We may think we have left our families behind and are not aware of the influence they have in our lives. For example, we may carry on a conversation with our parents in our minds. We imagine the way we might respond to our parents and they to us. We then may react to them as though the imagined family dialogue had actually taken place.

Sometimes we live our lives as though we are trying to prove something to our families. It is important that we are conscious of the influence of our families on us and that we work through as best we can the difficulties we experience within our families. The reason is that those who cut off contact with family are likely to repeat their troubled family relationships in their own marriages (Bowen, 1976, p. 84).

Let us look at an example of how families can affect a marriage. Don decided to drop out of law school and drive a truck while he decided what he really wanted to do in life. His father was a successful lawyer and had often pressured Don to be a lawyer and eventually become his partner. He was not sensitive to Don's different interests. When Don dropped out of school, his father was furious. After a nasty scene, Don left home and broke off all contact with his father. Occasionally, he called his mother. But he refused to talk with or about his father, and his father made no effort to get in touch with Don.

A year later, Don married Marilyn, who had dropped out of high school and was working as a waitress. The first three years of their marriage were happy. Don always put his work first, however. He had gone from driving a truck to starting his own trucking firm. Through a combination of hard work, smart business sense, and luck, the firm became quite successful. The more successful he was, the more Don seemed driven to do even better. His secret dream was to make a million dollars to show his father that he could become more successful than his father had ever dreamed of being. As he became more and more wrapped up in his business, Marilyn felt more and more alone. She seemed unable to get his attention. She decided on her own it was time to have a child, and became pregnant, thinking that a baby would bring Don home more. Instead, she found herself even more alone. She was tied down with all the responsibilities of a baby and unable even to join Don for lunch or dinner out as they had done in the past. Feeling unloved and unattractive, Marilyn was caught off guard by an old boyfriend who called her. She left the baby with a friend and had lunch with him to "talk about old times." This was the first of several meetings which led finally to her decision to divorce Don.

Even if the relationship with parents or brothers and sisters is so full of conflict and anger that it gives little support or love, it at least allows us to keep the conflict and anger between persons, where it needs to be, and not hidden away inside us. When it lurks somewhere inside, it can exert far more control over our lives than we recognize. By listening and understanding, and showing respect and support, we can keep the family conflict within its proper limits. Then we can work on strengthening the relationship that is important to both sides.

Friends.—Friends are also vital links in the web of support for a marriage. We may find it difficult to share friendships with our partners. The large part of our day is spent apart from each other. We tend to make our friends where we work because these are often the people with whom we share common interests. The wife who works as a homemaker also makes friends with the other wives and mothers who are a part of her circle of work. The result of making friends in our work circle is that our personal friends may be only slightly acquainted with our marital partner. Partners may even find themselves feeling jealous of the enjoyment we share with friends which does not include them. They may be jealous of our time spent with our co-workers.

We need personal friends. Personal friends can help us develop our individual gifts and enjoy special interests. A husband may have friends that enjoy going to ball games together which his wife hates to do. A wife may enjoy an exercise class with her friends. Marriage can be strengthened by such friendships.

With some effort, some personal friends may also become friends whom we share with our partner. Just as personal friends are important to us as individuals, shared friends are important to our marriage. Together we can find ways to share joy with one another as partners in the company of friends. Caring for and supporting our friends gives us a common purpose and shared meaning in our life. Friends can also help us keep our troubles in perspective. They can even challenge us to tackle the troubles in our marriage that we might otherwise ignore.

The ability to develop shared friendships is not just good for a marriage; it can be seen as a commandment we are given as Christians. Showing hospitality is an important virtue in the New Testament (Rom. 12:13; 1 Tim. 3:2; Titus 1:8; Heb. 13:2; 1 Pet. 4:9; and 3 John 5-6). Hospitality does not mean entertaining guests with a six-course meal of fatted calf or throwing gala parties. Hospitality is inviting someone home to share take-out Chinese food or a pot roast for Sunday dinner, even though the house is a mess. It is inviting the co-worker and her husband who just transferred in from another town to go to a ball game with us. Hospitality is making one's home an open place, where others can feel comfortable and accepted and enjoy being together. It also involves opening one's family life to the view of others. This requires that both partners be committed to the importance of sharing their home, their food, their time, and their relationship with others. From this kind of sharing, couples fulfill their calling as Christians and receive the blessing of shared friendships in return.

Church.—The church is not always a place where couples can immediately develop a web of vital relationships. A church may be so large that a couple can remain anonymous for months. They may never get to know anyone else very well, particularly if they attend only worship services. For those couples who become involved as participants and not just observers, the church can be a wonderful place to develop a web of supportive relationships. Churches that make it a point to include people in small groups where they can become more intimately acquainted with one another can facilitate this process. This enables a church to become truly a church family. It is a community in which people can find others to share with them both their joys and their burdens (Gal. 6:2; Rom. 12:15).

More often than not, couples whose marriages are in trouble either are not part of a church family or withdraw from the church's life. If they have been active members, they may feel uncomfortable about their troubled marriage. They may sense the judgment, either real or imaginary, of their fellow church members. They may withdraw or be forced to withdraw at the very time they need the church family the most. This is also the time when the church family needs to reach out with loving wisdom to the couple. While we need to respect the couple's privacy and the uniqueness of their situation, that does not mean that we allow troubled couples to withdraw silently to struggle alone with their problems.

To sum up, relationships with others can be a source of pain in marriage. Couples need not withdraw, however, from painful relationships, but should look for ways to restore and transform those relationships whenever possible. In addition, troubled couples need to make a strong effort *not* to do what might come naturally—pull away from family, friends, or church in the midst of the anger, embarrassment, or depression that may come with marital trouble. These are the very times that we need others to lend support and simply be there.

7

Can Our Broken Covenant Be Redeemed?

Someone has said, "Marriages are made in heaven—so are thunder and lightning." All marriage partners have to deal with conflict, with hurt, with disappointment in one another. Times come when partners have to confront one another with their broken covenant. Hosea's relationship with Gomer was filled with heartache and more heartache. Hosea's faithfulness in spite of Gomer's flings revealed the meaning of a covenant relationship (Hos. 3:1). A necessary ingredient for a covenant is the ability to forgive the other when he or she fails. As we forgive one another, we live out God's forgiveness of us (Matt. 18:33). Paul told us in Ephesians to "be kind to one another, tenderhearted, forgiving one another, as God in Christ forgave you" (4:32). This applies to marriage as well as to all Christian relationships.

When we can forgive one another, (1) we short-circuit the vicious circle of vengeance between us, (2) we recognize our own and our partner's responsibility for the hurt, (3) we repent, (4) we remember what has happened and make it a part of our shared history, and (5) we move on into the future together.

Stopping the Vicious Circle of Vengeance

When we forgive one another, we stop the endless cycle of returning hurt for hurt, insult for insult, rejection for rejection. The forgiving partner chooses not to strike back, to get even. In the Sermon on the Mount, Jesus told us to turn the other cheek (Matt. 5:39). This is even harder than it sounds. He says, "If any one strikes you on the *right* cheek, turn to him the other also" (authors' italics). The right cheek is specified. This does not mean that if someone slugs you on the left cheek, you are free to slug him back. Jesus is not talking about getting slugged at all. Think about hitting someone so that the blow lands on the right cheek. The left hand was considered unclean and would not have been used. To hit someone on the right cheek, one would have to use the back of the right hand. A blow to the right cheek, then, would be an insulting slap. Jesus is saying that when someone slaps you deliberately to humiliate you, turn the other cheek. The disciple is therefore to check the initial impulse to strike back when insulted. To retaliate is to begin a battle of fists or insults. In marriage, a partner who forgives—even deliberate hatefulness—looks toward rebuilding the relationship rather than revenge. A philosophy of an eye for an eye and a tooth for a tooth in marriage usually leads to a bloody mess.

With forgiveness, the healing process can begin. The forgiving partner says, "I am hurt and angry at you, but shouting insults at you or trying to get even with you is not going to help either of us or our marriage. I want us to learn what we can from what has happened, to change it, and to go on." Forgiveness is costly. It costs pride. It requires self-control. It takes a vision. For Christians, that vision comes from Christ's own example. Jesus forgave his enemies (1 Pet. 2:22-24) and commanded us to do the same, even to pray for them (Matt. 5:44). Sometimes a marriage partner can become our worst enemy. That partner knows our most vulnerable spots and can insult us and hurt us in ways no one else can. In forgiving, we take the first step toward turning the enemy back into a covenant partner. We change our relationship from a battleground into one of support and care.

By forgiving and praying for one another in the midst of hurt and conflict, we accomplish two things. First, we tap into the unmeasurable resources of God's grace and strength. Things we could not do alone become possible for us through God's power. Second, we change our focus. We no longer occupy ourselves with coming up with the "best" way to get even or with carefully rehearsing what we will say that will strike home and cause the most damage to our partner's self-esteem. When we pray for our partner, we have to think about our partner's needs and situation. This is the first step in offering understanding and respect for our partner. In the act of praying, we are transformed from an enemy launching deadly warheads to a covenant partner offering loving support.

Forgiveness in the New Testament is not offered with strings attached. We are not to forgive someone conditionally and say something like, "I'll forgive you this time if you swear you'll never do it again," or, "I'll give you one more chance." To offer forgiveness on the condition that the partner makes some change is not forgiveness at all: it is a contract. Forgiveness is not a business transaction. It is a gift. It mirrors God's grace (Eph. 5:1-2). We cannot earn God's grace with promises to do better or be nicer. We cannot bargain for it. God offers forgiveness freely. We should as well. When forgiveness is a contract, the marriage covenant shrinks to a contract also. Covenant partners can use contracts to try some new change in their relationship, but contracts cannot be the basis of their relationship. Love and forgiveness is not something they can negotiate.

As critical as stopping the cycle of vengeance is, forgiveness does not by itself restore the relationship between partners. It is simply the first step. The wife of an alcoholic may forgive her husband for the hurt, embarrassment, financial loss, and constant worry he causes. In forgiving him, she stops yelling, nagging, and doing things to get even with what he is doing to her. She accepts his problem and says, "I'm hurt and angry at what your drinking is doing to you and to us, but I recognize that my trying to make you change or get even with you is not going to help us." Although her forgiveness is a first step, they still have a long way to go.

The husband of a wife who has been caught in a sexual affair may say to her, "I feel betrayed, alone, and angry. But going out and having an affair myself to get back at you, or punishing you with silence or with yelling, or leaving you is not going to help us recover our marriage." To stop the cycle of hurt is the first step. It lays the foundation. The work of restoring the relationship must then begin.

Recognizing Responsibility

To forgive a marriage partner does not mean to ignore, tolerate, or excuse their hurtful behavior. Restoring the covenant between partners requires that each respect the other enough to hold them responsible for what they have done. We and our partners are each free to choose the paths that our lives will take. Whatever the reasons, our partners usually *choose* to do what they do. Powerful forces may be at work, but persons have some ability to control their own behavior. If they did not, partners would have no need to forgive one another. Instead, they would need simply to offer unconditional love to one another.

Let us look at the situation of two wives to explain what we mean. Both wives are an hour and a half late coming home on Saturday from a morning jog. Both husbands are very worried. Jane is late because she met a friend, and they stopped at a favorite bakery to have doughnuts and coffee. Marian is late because she twisted her ankle and had to walk home slowly and in a great deal of pain. No public phone is located nearby where she could have called her husband.

Obviously, Marian's husband does not need to forgive her for spraining her ankle. She had no choice in whether or not to be late and worry him. She may say, "I'm sorry I worried you," but she does not need forgiveness; she needs his love and concern. Jane's husband, on the other hand, now must choose whether to forgive Jane or not. She had a choice. She could have said to her friend, "No, I can't stop. It would worry my husband if I took so long to get home." Or she could have chosen to call him from the bakery. Instead, she chose to give little thought to how her actions would affect him. Jane is responsible for the choice she made.

Ignoring and Tolerating

Sometimes in troubled marriages, partners simply ignore the hurt or rips in their covenant. They choose the "peace at any price" route. Perhaps with an air of martyrdom, they go on about their daily lives, ignoring or putting up with their partners' behavior. Jane's husband, for example, may have said nothing about her being so late for fear of starting an argument. Other partners may ignore their spouses' extramarital affairs, or any number of the other ways that partners inflict pain on one another. Partners may fear that if they confront one another with the hurtful behavior, the conflict will be so great that the marriage may break apart.

Ignoring and tolerating a partner's sins against the marriage covenant, including such minor problems as Jane's thoughtlessness, is not forgiveness. God does not ignore or tolerate our sin. Forgiveness means to choose not to give the other what they deserve. But we cannot make the choice to forgive if we do not first recognize the behavior. Closing our eyes to the problem is not forgiveness; it is toleration or excusing.

If Jane's husband overlooks her thoughtlessness and swallows his own anger for the worry she caused him, he ignores an important warning sign in the marriage: his own feelings. He does not make her responsible for the trouble she has caused him. And it is unlikely she will do anything differently the next time. Nothing changes. No foundation is laid for them to begin together to tackle the trouble that has come between them. Even though this particular issue seems minor, it probably represents a larger problem.

Excusing

Excusing, like ignoring and tolerating, does not hold partners responsible for what has happened. We recognize what they have done, but we explain it away. We blame something else or someone else for what has happened.

For example, when Jane's husband learns that she had doughnuts with her friend, Denise, he explodes in a rage, "I cannot stand that Denise. She does not like me, and I know she is trying to break us up. She is a terrible influence on you since she left her husband. I don't want you to spend any more time with that woman!" Jane's husband has, in effect, said, "You aren't responsible for what you did—Denise is. You can't do anything to make it different. The problem is Denise." In saying this, he communicates a lack of respect for Jane. He treats her like a teenager who is so influenced by others that she cannot make free choices. Again, there is no forgiveness here, unless he were to forgive Denise! There is no change in their marriage either. As he has defined it, the problem is not located in their relationship but in Denise.

We often excuse one another in marriage. We may excuse a partner for leaving the bathroom or kitchen a mess—"He must have been in a real hurry this morning!" Or for forgetting to run an errand—"You have been under a lot of pressure lately; it is no wonder you are forgetful." Excusing is not forgiving, because it calls for no change. It simply offers the other loving acceptance. It is important to be able to excuse our partners every now and then. Times occur when all of us, because of personal weakness, fatigue, illness, stress, or a variety of other factors, need to be excused for being less than perfect.

Problems arise when we excuse something that requires forgiveness. Partners may not be able to ignore an extramarital affair, so they excuse it—"She was seduced by that rascal. He knew just how to take advantage of her." Excusing does not call for any change in our partner or in our marriage. Perhaps that is why we so easily excuse one another. By excusing each other, we do not have to face up to the troubles in our marriage. We do not have to confront how we have failed one another. And we do not have to make changes.

Repenting and Seeking Forgiveness from One Another

Forgiveness alone cannot restore the relationship between partners. Just as the "call to worship" is not the worship experience itself, forgiveness is the "call to restoration" but not the restoration. It is a signal that we will not seek vengeance, but offer love instead. Restoring the relationship between partners requires that one, and usually both, repent of the harm they have inflicted on one another. Only then can they begin the process of making changes that will rebuild their marriage.

Too often, partners take for granted the loyalty and love of their partner. They assume that the love offered by their partners gives them a blank check to do whatever they please and their marriage will survive. This is the way God's people, Israel, sometimes treated God. We can have our fun with other gods, and surely God will take us back.

It is usually not the tragedy of a sexual affair that destroys a

marriage, although that may be the last straw. It is the every-
day hurt and taking one another for granted that pecks away at
the foundation of love and leaves partners vulnerable to temptation. We are less polite and are grumpier with our partner
than with friends and work colleagues. We are more likely to
"take things out" on our partner than anyone else in our life.
We do this because we feel "safe" with our partner. If we acted
at work or with friends the way we act at home, we might
quickly find people spurning us. We act that way at home because we take our partner for granted. If we snarl at our partners, they are not immediately going to phone a divorce
lawyer. Although taking one another for granted does not spell
the end of a marriage, it contributes negatively to our life together. In time, it may build up resentment and distance between us. Our relationship will grow only as we care for each
other.

A number of years ago, the popular movie *Love Story* influenced many couples with its well-known line, "Love means
never having to say you are sorry." Such a statement assumes
that if people love one another, they will simply forget about
the hurts and problems that they inflict on one another. Saying
"I'm sorry" may not solve the problem. But repentance begins
with an "I'm sorry." Then one seeks not to repeat the behavior
that has hurt the loved one.

The prodigal son came to himself in the midst of a pig sty
when the hunger pangs made it clear that he had been a fool.
He returned to his father, practicing his confession every step
of the way, "Father, I have sinned against heaven and before
you; I am no longer worthy to be called your son; treat me as
one of your hired servants" (Luke 15:18-19). To his great surprise, the father ran to surround him with forgiveness before
he ever got the first word of "I'm sorry" out of his mouth. He
was then restored as a son, not as a hired hand, and treated

royally with a banquet. Everything seemed to be resolved. But if the son had lazed around the farm and continued to act irresponsibly, the "I'm sorry" would have meant nothing. If he was truly repentant, he would not break his father's heart again and would grab a hoe and help with the farm work. He needed to stay for more than a few free meals of fatted calf. He needed to take on the responsibilities that went with being a son to his father.

Covenant partners do not *owe* each other forgiveness. It is a gift freely offered. The father of the prodigal son did not have to forgive his son when he returned. Most would have thought it more prudent to take him on as a hired hand for a while, or at least put him on probation. The father chose, however, to give him the gift of forgiveness. Forgiveness is not a gift that can be demanded. We cannot say, "I know I have hurt you terribly, but, remember, you promised to love me for better or for worse!" In some ways, we are to our spouses as children are to a loving grandmother. They may hope for a surprise when she comes to visit; they may even come to expect it since she has been faithful to bring a surprise each time she comes. Yet it is still a gift, a surprise. To *ask* for the gift as soon as she arrives is not just bad manners. It says, "We want you to come see us only because you bring us surprises." The children have come to think she owes them surprises. Sensitive children quickly learn to communicate their love for Grandma and to take the surprises as surprises, not as their just due.

We can seek our partner's forgiveness. We cannot demand it as our right as a covenant partner. We can repent and change our hurtful ways *whether our partner forgives or not*. Just as forgiveness is offered without conditions, so is repentance. The elder brother of the prodigal son may never come to join the welcome-home party. He may never forgive his brother and always hold his foolish past over his head. But the repentant younger son cannot demand forgiveness from his brother, "Father says you had better forgive me, too!" He can change his behavior to show that his father was not wrong in taking him back as he did. In the same way, a loving partner does not wait for the spouse to make the first move in forgiveness. A loving partner does not wait for forgiveness to repent and begin again to live as a faithful and loving partner.

So far, we have talked as though it is one partner who does wrong and the other who forgives. Unfortunately, life is rarely that simple. Forgiveness usually needs to be mutual. That is because we often have both hurt one another. Because our lives are so intertwined, we are one of the significant forces in each other's life that influence what we do. We are each responsible for what we do as individuals. But it may be the case that we may have been more of a problem for our partner than a support. The unfaithful spouse, for example, must repent from the choice to break the marriage covenant if the marriage is to continue. On the other side, the other partner may need to repent from the hostile anger and punishing silence that helped to create a climate in which unfaithfulness became an attractive choice. If we really commit ourselves to looking at what has happened and at what needs to change so that our future will be different, it may mean that both partners need to repent and rectify their behavior.

Forgiveness does not restore the relationship; repentance also is required. It takes two persons to make a relationship. When the father of the prodigal son saw his wayfaring son on the horizon, he ran to hug and kiss him. In that day, it was undignified for an elder to run. As we noted before, this took place before the son ever got out his repentance speech he had been practicing (v. 20). It was a sign of forgiveness before forgiveness had been asked. But the relationship could not be restored simply because the father had forgiven his son. The son had to come home.

We can forgive someone who does not repent, but it does not restore the relationship. As covenant partners, spouses need to forgive whether their partners repent or not. Their forgiveness, however, is not enough to restore a broken covenant.

Redemptive Remembering

Forgiveness and repentance do not mean that we say to one another "let's just forget it ever happened." In the parable of the unforgiving servant, a king forgave a huge debt owed him by one of his servants when the servant pleaded with him for mercy. Smiling at his good fortune, the servant then met a fellow servant who owed him, by comparison, only a trifling sum. Instead of sharing the forgiveness he had experienced, the servant refused to listen to the debtor's pleas. He grabbed the poor fellow by the scruff of the neck and had him thrown into jail. When the king heard what had happened, he was angry: "Then his lord summoned him and said to him, 'You wicked servant! I forgave you all that debt because you besought me; and should not you have had mercy on your fellow servant, as I had mercy on you?' " (Matt. 18:32-33).

The king did not forgive and forget. He remembered having forgiven the huge debt and called him to task. Forgiving does not mean forgetting. We forgive our marriage partners. We do not expect them to repay us or make up in some way for what they have done. But when we forgive, we expect their behavior to be different in the future. Forgiveness is not a blanket pardon that allows the partner to continue unchanged. Forgiveness may be offered freely; but to accept it, to repent, requires that we make some change.

In Jesus' parable, remembering the forgiveness is the responsibility of the one who has been forgiven. The king expected the *servant* to remember the forgiveness he had experienced. Remembering is a part of repentance.

In the book *Forgive and Forget,* Lewis Smedes calls this "redemptive remembering." In the wilderness wandering, Moses taught the Israelites to remember what they had experienced. This included the good and bad memories. They needed to remember their own sin, God's forgiveness, and the renewal of their covenant. As Christians, we celebrate God's forgiveness, our repentance, and our covenant with God through Christ's atoning sacrifice each time we partake of the Lord's Supper. These are vital parts of our continuing walk in covenant with our Lord.

In the same way, couples need to remember the times of forgiveness, repentance, and renewal of their covenant with one another. Our repentance and forgiveness form vital pieces of our shared history. They give our covenant roots and strength. We can look back together at the storms we have endured together. To forget the hurt, the forgiveness, and the repentance in our past means there is nothing to stop us from repeating the destructive behavior. "Forgive and forget" has no place in a covenant relationship.

Moving On Together into the Future

Fairness concentrates on the past; forgiveness focuses on the future (Garland & Garland, 1986, p. 122). When we try to be fair to each other, we constantly look back. We keep books on what each has received and try to even the score. Our remembering is "score remembering." We keep a tally in our head of how many strikes each partner has against them. Forgiveness, on the other hand, is "redemptive remembering." We do not keep track of the strikes as much as we do the forgiveness and repentance that followed the strikeouts.

The remembering of forgiveness and repentance allow us to celebrate our past. It does not permit us to beat one another over the head with it. It is the encouragement to go on into whatever storms face us ahead. Our past mistakes do not become a burden that will weigh us down the rest of our lives. We may carry the scars of our relationship proudly. We do not pretend that they do not exist, because they show that, with God's help, we have been able to heal the hurts between us. We can face the future having learned from each other, having grown and changed and matured through the trials we have experienced together, and with a tough love for one another that can stand up to serious challenge.

8

Is There Christian
Life After Divorce?

It takes two to tango and two to make a relationship. But just as one partner can ruin a dance by tromping all over the other's feet, one partner can singlehandedly destroy a marriage. In the last chapter, we talked about forgiveness being the first step in restoring the covenant between marital partners. If forgiveness is not met by the repentance of the other partner, the forgiving spouse alone cannot make a marriage work. Covenants, including marriage covenants, by definition require two persons to choose freely to commit themselves to one another. For one partner to try to continue a marriage after the other has emotionally pulled out is like one hand trying to clap by itself.

Paul knew that one spouse cannot make a marriage work. In his Letter to the Corinthians, he recognized that sometimes a partner no longer "consents to" continuing in a marriage (1 Cor. 7:12-13). He wrote, "If the unbelieving partner desires to separate, let it be so" (v. 15). Paul knew that divorce is not what God intends for us, but he also knew that God has called us to peace (v. 15; Rom. 12:18; 14:19). Trying to cling desperately to a relationship that one partner is determined to dissolve will only bring more problems. Unfortunately, divorce is the only route to peace.

In other cases, divorce does not occur because one spouse has chosen to end the marriage covenant, but because both have decided that divorce is the only solution. What can be said concerning Christians who decide to divorce?

Deciding to Divorce

No one chooses divorce gladly. No matter how destructive and painful a marriage may have been, divorce is still a wrenching experience (Berscheid, 1983). Even if a husband and wife fought like cats and dogs, they have developed patterns of living that include each other. They have bonded together. Like two plants growing in the same pot, their roots have become so intertwined that separation tears and destroys part of each.

Deciding to divorce is an agonizing process. It is also a lonely process. The Bible deals with the question of divorce and offers guidance for Christians struggling with this decision. Persons considering divorce also need to know what generally happens when couples decide on divorce. This knowledge can help them make their own decision.

What Does the Bible Say About Divorce?

In the times in which the Bible was written, divorce was not a decision granted by a divorce court judge. The husband simply decided to divorce his wife. The law of Moses required only that the husband give his wife a bill of divorce. This made her free to become the wife of another man. It also forbade the first husband from remarrying her after she had become the wife of another who then divorced her or died (Deut. 24:1-4). The written bill of divorce gave the wife some protection. She could not be accused of adultery if she remarried. Forbidding the husband to remarry her also protected her from her first husband interfering in her second marriage.

In the law of Moses, divorce is taken for granted as a fact of life that needed some controls. The law does not say whether divorce is good or bad, or whether one should divorce or not. It does not give the grounds for divorce. A wife may have done something unseemly, or the husband simply may not want her anymore (if the husband "dislikes" her, Deut. 24:3). Whatever the reason, the law concerns itself with what happens when the husband has decided to divorce his wife. If he chooses to divorce her, he must provide her with a divorce certificate and may never remarry her after she has married another. The latter, and not divorce, was considered to be the abomination.

In Jesus' day, men assumed that they had the right to divorce their wives. The wife belonged to the husband just like any other property he might possess. A husband could dispose of his property as he chose, and this applied to his wife. If a husband brought false charges of adultery against his wife, or if he had been forced to marry her because he had violated her virginity, however, he was not allowed to divorce her (Deut. 22:13-19,28-29).

Wives, on the other hand, had no right to divorce their husbands. Only for special reasons could they bring a divorce suit: their husbands had a skin disease or morbid growth, worked at a disgusting trade that made them stink (dung collector or tanner), or were impotent.

Jesus, however, turned this culturally accepted practice on its head. He stated flatly that marriage was designed by God to be a lifelong commitment. He concluded, "What therefore God has joined together, let not man put asunder" (Matt. 19:6; Mark 10:9). In Matthew 19:8, Jesus explained that Moses did not command husbands to give a certificate of divorce; he *permitted* it because theirs hearts were hard. In other words, he allowed divorce because of their sinfulness. It was a concession to sin.

Up to this point, husbands could feel righteous so long as they followed the proper procedures—giving the wife her legal

divorce certificate. Having done exactly what Moses commanded, they thought that they could safely ignore what
God's intention for marriage was in the beginning. They also
thought they could ignore the effect of their action on others.
They had followed the law to the letter. But for Jesus, this was
never adequate. They had ignored the spirit of the law, God's
will for marriage. God desires mercy, not legally correct certif-
icates. Therefore, Jesus said one cannot divorce one's wife and
be righteous before God. It might be lawful, but it is still bad.
The husband thinks that he is the lord of the marriage when he
discards his wife like a piece of used property. But God joined
the couple together, and God is the real Lord of the marriage.
Therefore, whoever breaks their marriage covenant will have
to answer to God.

Jesus taught that, in the beginning, God gave marriage to
humans as a good gift (Matt. 19:4-5). God's will was that there
be no divorce. When marriages fail, therefore, partners have
failed to live according to God's will. They have, in effect,
rejected God's good gift. There is no getting around this (see
also 1 Cor. 7:12-16). But we should recognize that when Jesus
condemned divorce in Matthew 19:3-10 (see also Mark 10:2-
12), He was responding to a bunch of men who were trying to
trick Him. They were convinced that they were righteous.
They thought they could divorce their wives and still appear
righteous before God because they had painted by the num-
bers in their legal process. But they were in truth evil men who
would dump a wife and plot Jesus' death without any qualms.
Jesus challenged them to recognize the significance of the marital covenant. He also made clear that joining together to make
one flesh is God's will. Tearing asunder is man's will.

It is important to note that when Jesus made these statements about divorce, He was *not* speaking to marital partners
struggling with a crumbling marriage. He was speaking to His

opponents. His intention was to set the record straight for these self-righteous hypocrites about what God thinks about divorce. As the prophet Malachi said, "[God] hates divorce" (Mal. 2:13-16). God hates divorce because of what it does to persons. It is destructive to both partners and to their children. It turns God's good gift of marriage into a vale of tears. But God does not hate the devorced person. God hates sin because, like cancer, it destroys persons. But God seeks to heal the sinner.

Sinners do not need condemnation by us; they need grace and healing. When the Pharisees saw Jesus eating with the wrong crowd, they said, "[These are] tax collectors and sinners!" Jesus said, in effect, "I know." "Those who are well have no need of a physician, but those who are sick. Go and learn what this means, 'I desire mercy, and not sacrifice.' For I came not to call the righteous, but sinners" (Matt. 9:10-13). Sometimes the church has acted like the Pharisees and has said, "But these are divorced persons." Just so, they are the ones in particular need of the Physician's balm. Divorce is a sin. It is not unforgivable, however. It will always leave scars, but God wills to heal the wounds we inflict on ourselves.

What Happens When Couples Divorce

Divorce does not end the relationship between partners, although it may end their covenant.—Sometimes people are shocked to find that divorce does not end their marital troubles. Relationships do not begin and end with legal actions. The marriage relationship may no longer be visible, but it remains, nevertheless. Even if partners never have any more contact with one another after the divorce, they carry in their own lives the effects of the marriage. Each is different because of the time and commitment they shared. The only way to end a relationship completely is to develop a good case of amnesia.

When a couple has children, this is even more the case. The partners may no longer be spouses, but they are still parenting partners. Divorce does not cancel the bond of parenting (Atkin & Rubin, 1976). The continuing relationship of parents with each other after divorce is very important for the children. This relationship is far more important to children, in fact, than whether their parents are legally married or not. When one parent leaves and cuts off ties with the children as well as with the spouse, everyone suffers, particularly the children (Ahrons, 1983).

Most divorced persons who are parents, therefore, continue to have regular contact with their former spouses. They have to arrange schedules for visits. They share the costs for the children's upbringing. They may both attend a Little League game, a piano recital, or a school graduation. Many consider former spouses to be friends. In fact, they may become better friends than when they were married. And some may even share more time with one another than is required by coordinating their parenting (Ahrons, 1980).

Divorce places new limits on the relationship between partners.—Even though divorce does not end the relationship, it does alter it. Although it is not uncommon for former spouses to continue to have sexual relations with one another, this part of the relationship gradually disappears (Weiss, 1975). Outward signs, such as changed residences and lack of legal and personal responsibility for one another reflect the inner changes in how each thinks of the other.

Some of these limits are key reasons for why partners may have sought divorce. The spouse of an alcoholic, for example, may now have legal ways to protect financial resources from an irresponsible partner. The physically abused spouse is now protected from further violence by court action.

In some respects, these new limits represent a transformation in the marriage from a covenant relationship to a contract relationship, enforceable by the sheriff's department, if necessary. The relationship continues, but it now has clear conditions and expectations. This process of transformation may never be completed, however. Former spouses may continue to offer support, love, and understanding to one another that resembles more the covenant of a marriage or friendship than it does a contract.

Divorce does not change the individual troubles that caused the marital problems. It may, however, change other troubles for better or for worse.—We walk out of a marriage with the same personal problems that plagued us in the marriage. If we were insecure, depressed, and unhappy with ourselves in the marriage, it is not likely that divorce will bring much change for the better in how we feel about ourselves.

Other troubles may be transformed. For example, divorce usually brings an end to patterns of open, unending conflict. Partners now live their own lives without having to struggle through conflicting values and belief with one another. Partners also have to learn to do things—from paying bills to cooking—that were the former spouse's responsibilities.

Divorce brings with it dramatic changes in the world around the couple. Even if a divorce is friendly, shared friends often feel forced to choose sides. This means that spouses lose many of the very friends that they may need for support through this critical time. Family relationships are also thrown into turmoil. The extended family faces grief over the broken marriage. The former spouse's family suddenly seems "off limits," even though they may have become very important parts of a person's life. Some stresses also become even worse. Money and the lack of it becomes a real source of stress, particularly for women. Most women come out of divorce much poorer than they were in the marriage, particularly if they have custody of their children. At a time when persons need particular support and love from friends and family, and perhaps more money than usual to set up a new home as a single person, they may find these resources shrinking dramatically because of the divorce.

Divorce may end the conflict and hurt between couples and may even highlight the positive aspects of their relationship. It may also do just the opposite.—During the process of deciding to divorce, persons often focus on the problems in the marriage. By doing this, they confirm their commitment to the hard decision they are making. After the process of grief over the lost marriage begins, they are struck by all the good things about the marriage they had shoved into the backs of their minds when they were talking themselves into the divorce. Only after the divorce do they begin to recall the enjoyable parts of the marriage. This often brings with it some regret and the wish that the marriage could be restored. When we are frightened at the prospect of facing the future alone, the security of the past marriage may look very appealing.

On the other hand, a couple may have decided in a fairly friendly way to end their marriage. They commit themselves to continue to be friends and to try not to hurt one another any further. The legal process, however, may bring out hidden anger. It can give spouses an excuse for fighting to get what they can from the other—financial assets, rights to the children, and so on. The result is that they try to achieve a victory over one another much more than they try to support one another.

Divorce begins a process of grief and a reordering of life.— It is common for persons to waltz through a separation and divorce; they pat themselves on the back for having weathered such a dramatic change so well. Then they plunge into depression. Life now has to be completely reorganized without the other. It is a time of crisis. No matter how much partners hated or hurt one another when they were married, divorce brings grief. If they do not grieve over what was, then they grieve over dashed dreams of what might have been.

Christian Life After Divorce

Just as every marriage is unique, so is every divorce. For a few, divorce can be a blessing and a reminder of God's goodness in extending grace to us and allowing us new beginnings. For most, divorce is a devastating experience which casts a black cloud over life for years to come. For the Christian, divorce may be an experience in which we come face-to-face with ourselves and with God in a new way. It can force us to recognize afresh our weaknesses and our need for a Heavenly Father. The Christian who is moving on from divorce needs to:

Understand What Happened

The Christian needs to look at self, not just the partner, to understand what happened. Divorce is easy to blame on the partner. The partner is not there, after all, to provide his or her own defense. Blaming, however, takes us off the hook. We may say to ourselves, "What happened wasn't my fault." But it is rarely true. The troubles which led up to divorce usually are the mutual responsibility of both partners. If we are willing to hold a mirror up to see our own part in the breakdown of the relationship, we are likely to find something we need to learn and perhaps change about ourselves.

Learn From What Happened and End
the Sin Against One Another

To divorce someone does not mean we no longer have to forgive the other or repent for the hurt we caused in our relationship. Former partners who carry with them the pain and anger they have toward each other, and who are unwilling to forgive, will continue to allow the marriage to distort their lives. We must remember Jesus' commandment to love and forgive our enemies. Jesus said nothing about forgiving people only if we are going to continue to be in a relationship with them. Forgiveness is required of us as Christians as a sign of God's forgiveness of us. Forgiveness may not be able to heal the broken covenant, but it can heal the wounds within us. Anger is a warning signal to alert us to the relationship problems. The relationship is now broken. The anger can serve no good purpose. If we allow it to fester, however, it can destroy us and hurt others, including our children.

In the same way, we need to repent from the hurt and destruction we ourselves caused, whether or not the former partner offers forgiveness. Perhaps the patterns in our relationship that needed change are now shattered. It may be too late for changes. Nevertheless, the shadows of our behavior in the former marriage remain a part of our lives. For example, it may do little to salvage the marriage if we change our pattern of blaming the marriage partner for all the problems in our marriage and refusing to try to understand the partner's side of things. We may find, however, that our patterns of relating to our teenage children are no different. This can lead to a breakdown in our relationship with our children. Repentance means, then, that we will begin to try more respectful, loving ways of sharing our feelings with our teenagers, ways that will build our relationship with them, not destroy it.

Forgiveness and repentance may still have a very important role to play in healing the continuing relationship we may have with our ex-spouse. We have already talked about the significant ways in which our relationship with one another will continue even after divorce. That relationship need not continue the destructive, painful patterns.

Claim God's Promises for New Life

As Christians, we know that God offers us a chance to begin again when we have failed miserably. We cannot forget or ignore what we have experienced. We cannot undo what has been done. We will always bear the scars of a broken covenant. We should also carry with us the wisdom that comes from living through and overcoming life crises.

God always holds out the promises of a new life through Jesus Christ. We should remember that nothing can separate us from the love of God, not tribulation or distress—even the tribulation and distress of divorce.

Use What Has Been Learned About Personal Pain and Making Hard Decisions in Ministry with Others

When we pray, seeking God's presence in the lonely times and hard decisions of life, we have the assurance that God understands. We are not alone in our suffering. Jesus, too, was lonely, discouraged, misunderstood, used, and abused by others. Jesus, too, felt the sting of loved ones who betrayed Him, deserted Him, and denied Him. Jesus understands when this happens to us because He has been there.

One of the ways we witness to God's love is to show that love in our relationships with others. Divorced persons have a door open to them to witness to others struggling with fractured marriage covenants and the decision of divorce. They can understand, as others may not, the grief, uncertainty, anger, and fear when one faces life alone after divorce.

This does not mean that divorced persons now have all of the answers. Christians who have experienced divorce can offer understanding and support to others who badly need it in the lonely process of divorce. They can also offer their own experiences as information for others. Only the persons who are struggling with this problem can decide whether or not the experiences of others apply to their own life. In chapter 6, we talked about some ways we can keep the stresses and crises in our lives from swamping us. One way, you will remember, is to find meaning and purpose in the troubles we face. Divorce can be one of the greatest crises we ever face. It does not have to sink us, however. Divorce may only make some more bitter. Others may turn it into a more productive experience. If we are shaken from old patterns and have made important personal changes, divorce can become a constructive experience. If we find ways to minister to others faced with similar problems, the destructive force of divorce can be transformed into something redemptive and life-giving.

Begin Anew, A Changed Person

We recognize that we can never go back and erase what has happened in our life. One of the most difficult questions Christians face as they move on from divorce is whether or not they can begin a new relationship, and perhaps a new marriage covenant, and be faithful to their commitment to Christ. The problem is that Jesus said, "Every one who divorces his wife and marries another commits adultery" (Luke 16:18; see also Mark 10:11-12; Matt. 19:9). Adultery refers to a violation of the marriage bond. Jesus was saying, in effect, that the one-flesh relationship cannot be dissolved by a certificate of divorce. The reason He says this is to affirm that God intended marriage to be a lifetime commitment. Jesus is not trying to brand anyone as an adulterer. Those who use Jesus' words to condemn the remarried as adulterers should be mindful that Jesus also said that *anyone* who looks at another with lust commits adultery in the heart. We are all sinners. Some have sinned in different ways. Adultery is a sin. Divorce is a sin, but sin is forgivable. When Jesus met the Samaritan woman at the well, He knew that she had had five husbands and was living with one who was not her husband. He did not call her an adulteress but, instead, offered her an invitation to drink from

His living water. He gave her a chance to begin life renewed.
When Jesus was face-to-face with the woman caught in adultery, He did not condemn her as the others gathered around
did who were eagerly waiting to cast the second stone, if not
the first. Instead, He let her accusers know that they were no
better than she when it came to sin and told her to go and sin
no more. That did not mean she had to retreat to a convent;
she could start life again. This would suggest that one who has
failed in marriage does get another chance.

A broken marriage covenant does not fulfill God's intention,
but that is true of all sin. Divorced persons do not have to remain single the rest of their lives to avoid still more sin by remarrying. Divorce is not the one sin that does not allow us a
second chance. To apply Jesus' teaching about divorce as a legal principle by which to measure all persons is to ignore Jesus'
ministry to people. Jesus dealt with the needs of individuals as
foremost. He spoke out against bending people to fit laws.
Marriage was made for the benefit of persons, and not persons
for the marriage laws. It would seem, then, that a failed marriage should not block a future opportunity to enter again into
a covenant of marriage.

It is easy for persons who have never experienced divorce to
feel superior and sit in judgment of those who have. They
should be mindful that the covenant between partners does not
consist of a piece of paper filed away in some courthouse. It is
the love and loyalty they give to one another. This means that
every married person has at some time fractured the marriage
covenant in some way, with broken commitments, destructive
anger, or selfish use of the partner. We are not to pass judgment on others (Matt. 7:1-5).

A confused student was reported to have written in an essay
that Socrates died from an overdose of wedlock (instead of
hemlock). That may seem an apt description for those who feel

that their troubled marriage is poisoning the life out of them. They may see divorce as the only alternative. Divorce is not the end of the world. It may sever a marriage relationship, but it does not sever one's relationship to Christ.

A troubled marriage, however, need not lead inevitably to a parting of the ways. All couples experience troubles of one sort or another during their married life. The key to preventing the troubles from accumulating into a deadly overdose is to face them as partners committed to one another and to imparting the grace of God to one another, even in the midst of difficulty (Eph. 5:29).

In this book, we have attempted to offer help in understanding the causes of marital strife and some suggestions for overcoming it. We hope that it is useful to you, our readers, in the crises you face yourselves and in your ministry with others who are in the midst of crises. It is our prayer that this book will provide you with a new sense of hope for marriage and a new vision of God working in and through the covenant between partners.

References

Achtemeier, Elizabeth. 1976. *The committed marriage*. Philadelphia: Westminster.

Ahrons, Constance R. 1983. Divorce: Before, during, and after. In Hamilton I. McCubbin and Charles R. Figley (Eds.), *Stress and the family: Vol. 1. Coping with normative transitions*. New York: Brunner/Mazel.

Anderson, Carol. 1982. The community connection: The impact of social networks on family and individual functioning. In Froma Walsh (Ed.), *Normal family processes*. New York: Guilford Press.

Argyle, Michael, and Furnham, Adrian. 1983. Sources of satisfaction and conflict in long-term relationships. *Journal of Marriage and the Family, 45,* 481-93.

Atkin, Edith, and Rubin, Estelle. 1976. *Part-time father*. New York: Vanguard Press.

Bakely, Donald C. 1985. *Bethy and the mouse*. Newton, Kansas: Faith and Life Press.

Barth, M. 1974. *Ephesians*. The Anchor Bible. Garden City, N.Y.: Doubleday & Co.

Bernard, Jessie. 1982. *The future of marriage*, 2nd ed. New Haven, Conn.: Yale University Press.

Berscheid, Ellen. 1983. Emotion. In Harold H. Kelley and others (Eds.), *Close relationships*. New York: W. H. Freeman.

Bowen, Murray. 1976. Principles and techniques of multiple family therapy. In Philip J. Guerin (Ed.), *Family therapy: Theory and practice*. New York: Gardner Press.

Campbell, A., Converse, P., and Rogers, W. 1976. *The quality of American life*. New York: Russell Sage Foundation.

Cleek, Margaret Guminski, and Pearson, T. Allan. 1985. Perceived causes of divorce: An analysis of interrelationships. *Journal of Marriage and the Family, 47,* 179-83.

Duck, Steve. 1982. *Personal relationships 4: Dissolving personal relationships*. London: Academic Press.

Elkind, David. 1981. The family and religion. In Nick Stinnett and others, eds., *Family strengths 3: Roots of well-being*. Lincoln, NE: University of Nebraska Press.

Erbes, Janine Twomey, and Hedderson, John J. Cunneen. 1984. A longitudinal examination of the separation/divorce process. *Journal of Marriage and the Family*, 46, 937-41.

Garland, David E. 1987. The Biblical view of divorce. *Review and Expositor*, *84*, 461-72.

Garland, Diana S. R. 1987. Myths about marriage enrichment and implications for family ministry. In Herbert G. Lingren and others (Eds.), *Family strengths 8-9: Pathways to well-being*. Lincoln: University of Nebraska-Lincoln.

Garland, Diana S. R., and Garland, David E. 1986. *Beyond companionship: Christians in marriage*. Philadelphia: Westminster Press.

Garland, Diana S. R., and Hassler, Betty. 1987. *Covenant marriage*. Nashville: Sunday School Board.

Glenn, N. D., and Weaver, C. N. 1978. A multivariate multisurvey study of marital happiness. *Journal of Marriage and the Family*, 40, 549-56.

Gray, J. D., Cutler, C. A., Dean, J. G., and Kempe, C. H. 1979. Prediction and prevention of child abuse and neglect. *Journal of Social Issues*, 35, 127-39.

Guernsey, Dennis B. 1984. *The family covenant: Love and forgiveness in the Christian home*. Elgin, Ill.: David C. Cook Publishing Co.

Harriman, L. C. 1986. Marital adjustment as related to personal and marital changes accompanying parenthood. *Family Relations*, 35, 233-39.

Kaplan, Helen Singer. 1974. *The new sex therapy: Active treatment of sexual dysfunctions*. New York: Brunner/Mazel.

Kitson, Gay C., and Rashke, Helen J. 1981. Divorce research: What we know; what we need to know. *Journal of Divorce*, 4, 1-37.

Kotelchuck, M. 1982. Child abuse and neglect: Prediction and classification. In R. Starr (Ed.), *Child abuse prediction*. Cambridge, MA: Ballinger.

Larson, Jeffry H. 1984. The effect of husband's unemployment on marital and family relations in blue-collar families. *Family Relations*, *33*, 503-11.

Lemley, Brad. 1986. Biodance. *The Family Therapy Networker*. May-June, 15-16.

Lewis, Jerry M. 1979. *How's your family?* New York: Brunner/Mazel.

Lewis, Jerry M., and Looney, John G. 1983. *The long struggle: Well-functioning working-class black families*. New York: Brunner/Mazel.

Lewis, Lionel S., and Brissett, Dennis. 1977. Sex as work: A study of avocational counseling. In James E. DeBurger (Ed.), *Marriage today: Problems, issues, and alternatives*. New York: John Wiley & Sons.

Luckey, E. B., and Bain, J. K. 1970. Children: A factor in marital satisfaction. *Journal of Marriage and the Family*, 32, 43-44.

Mace, David R. 1982. *Love and anger in marriage*. Grand Rapids: Zondervan Publishing House.

Masters, William H., and Johnson, Virginia E. 1966. *Human sexual response*. Boston: Little, Brown & Co.

McCubbin, Hamilton I., and Patterson, Joan M. 1983. Family transitions: Adaptation to stress. In Hamilton I. McCubbin and Charles R. Figley (Eds.), *Stress and the family: Vol. I. Coping with normative transitions*. New York: Brunner/Mazel.

Meichenbaum, Donald, and Turk, Dennis. 1976. The cognitive-behavioral management of anxiety, anger, and pain. In Park O. Davidson (Ed.), *The behavioral management of anxiety, depression and pain*. New York: Brunner/Mazel.

Melville, Keith. 1980. *Marriage and family today*, 2nd ed. New York: Random House.

Miller, Sherod, Nunnally, Elam W., and Wackman, Daniel B. 1979. *Couple communication I: Talking together*. Minneapolis: Interpersonal Communication Programs, 1979.

Newberger, E., Reed, P., Danial, J., Hyde, J., and Kotelchuck, M. 1977. Pediatric social illness: Toward an etiologic classification. *Pediatrics*, 60, 178-85.

Pettit, Ellen J., and Bloom, Bernard L. 1984. Whose decision was it? The effects of initiator status on adjustment to marital disruption. *Journal of Marriage and the Family*, 46, 587-95.

Pilisuk, Marc, and Parks, Susan Hillier. 1983. Social support and family stress. *Marriage and Family Review*, 6, 137-56.

Pittman, Frank. 1984. Into the volcano. *The Family Therapy Networker*, 8, 63-65.

Renne, K. S. 1970. Correlates of dissatisfaction in marriage. *Journal of Marriage and the Family*, 32, 54-56.

Rollins, B. C., and Galligan, R. 1978. The developing child and marital satisfaction of parents. In R. M. Lerner and G. B. Spanier (Eds.), *Child influences on marital and family interaction*. New York: Academic Press, 1978.

Russell, C. S. 1974. Transition to parenthood: Problems and gratifications. *Journal of Marriage and the Family*, 36, 294-302.

Ryder, R. G. 1973. Longitudinal data relating marriage satisfaction and having a child. *Journal of Marriage and the Family*, 35, 604-606.

Sager, Clifford J., and others. 1983. *Treating the remarried family*. New York: Brunner/Mazel.

Sakenfeld, Katharine D. 1985. *Faithfulness in action: Loyalty in Biblical perspective*. Philadelphia: Fortress.

Satir, Virgina. 1972. *Peoplemaking*. Palo Alto: Science and Behavior Books, Inc.

Saxton, Lloyd. 1980. *The individual, marriage, and the family*, 4th ed. Belmont, CA: Wadsworth.

Skolnick, Arlene, and Skolnick, Jerome H. 1980. Introduction: Family in transition. In Arelen Skolnick and Jerome H. Skolnick, eds. *Family in transition*, 3rd ed. Boston: Little, Brown & Co.

Smedes, Lewis B. 1984. *Forgive and forget: Healing the hurts we don't deserve*. New York: Harper & Row.

Smith, Shirley M. 1983. Disaster: Family disruption in the wake of disaster. In Charles R. Figley and Hamilton I. McCubbin (Eds.), *Stress and the family: Vol. II. Coping with catastrophe*. New York: Brunner/Mazel.

Spanier, G., Lewis, R., and Cole, C. 1975. Marital adjustment over the family life cycle: The issue of curvilinearity. *Journal of Marriage and the Family*, 37, 263-75.

Straus, Marray A., Gelles, R. J., and Steinmetz, S. K. 1980. *Behind closed doors: Violence in the American family*. Garden City, N.Y.: Doubleday & Co.

Tavris, Carol. 1982. *Anger: The misunderstood emotion*. New York: Simon & Schuster.

Thielicke, Helmut. 1961. *How the world began*. Translation and introduction by John W. Doberstein. Philadelphia: Fortress Press.

Thompson, Linda, and Spanier, Graham B. 1983. The end of marriage and acceptance of marital termination. *Journal of Marriage and the Family*, 45, 103-13.

Tolstedt, B. E., and Stokes, J. P. 1983. Relation of verbal, affective, and physical intimacy to marital satisfaction. *Journal of Counseling Psychology*, 30, 573-80.

Vaughan, Diane. 1986. *Uncoupling: turning points in intimate relationships*. New York: Oxford University Press.

Visher, Emily B., and Visher, John S. 1979. *Step-families: A guide to working with stepparents & stepchildren*. New York: Brunner/ Mazel.

Voydanoff, Patricia. 1983. Unemployment: Family strategies for adaptation. In Charles R. Figley and Hamilton I. McCubbin (Eds.), *Stress and the family: Vol. II. Coping with catastrophe*. New York: Brunner/Mazel.

Wasserman, Ira M. 1984. A longitudinal analysis of the linkage between suicide, unemployment, and marital dissolution. *Journal of Marriage and the Family*, 46, 853-59.

Weiss, Robert S. 1975. *Marital separation*. New York: Basic Books.

White, Stephen W., and Bloom, Bernard L. 1981. Factors related to the adjustment of divorcing men. *Family Relations*, 30, 349-60.

DATE DUE

APR 0 5 2010		